D0430825

BISON
BOOKS

# Shantytown Kid

[ *Le Gone du Chaâba* ]

AZOUZ BEGAG

Edited and with an introduction by
Alec G. Hargreaves | Translated by
Naïma Wolf and Alec G. Hargreaves

*University of Nebraska Press* | *Lincoln and London*

Publication of this book was
NATIONAL assisted by a grant from the
ENDOWMENT
FOR THE ARTS National Endowment for the Arts.

*A Great Nation Deserves Great Art*

*Library of Congress
Cataloging-in-Publication Data*
Begag, Azouz, 1957–
[Gone du Chaâba. English]
Shantytown kid = Le gone du Chaâba
/ Azouz Begag; edited and with an
introduction by Alec G. Hargreaves;
translated by Naïma Wolf and Alec G.
Hargreaves.  p.  cm.
Includes bibliographical references.
ISBN-13:978-0-8032-6258-4 (pbk.: alk. paper)
ISBN-10: 0-8032-6258-2 (pbk.: alk. paper)
I. Harbreaves, Alec G.   II. Wolf, Naïma.
III. Title.   IV. Title: Gone du Chaâba.
PQ2662.E343G6613   2007
843'.914—dc22
2006050196

Set in Minion by Bob Reitz.
Designed by A. Shahan.

# Contents

*List of Illustrations*     vii

Introduction     ix

Shantytown Kid
[*Le Gone du Chaâba*]     1

*Glossaries and Guide
to Nonstandard
Pronunciation of French*     201

*Books and Articles
about Azouz Begag
and "Beur" Literature*     209

# Illustrations

*Map*

    Lyon, France          xxiii

*Photographs*

    Azouz Begag with
    his parents, 1965      xxv

    Azouz Begag,
    minister for equal
    opportunities, 2005    xxvii

# Introduction

*Alec G. Hargreaves*

On June 2, 2005, Azouz Begag received a phone call from France's newly appointed prime minister, Dominique de Villepin, inviting him to join the government. Begag agreed to serve as minister for equal opportunities. A week later, for his first official ministerial visit, he traveled to the city of Lyon, where decades earlier his parents, immigrants from Algeria, had raised him and the rest of their family in a shantytown they called Le Chaâba. Their poverty and social marginalization were typical of the living conditions experienced by Algerians in France. Like most immigrants from North Africa, where they had lived under French colonial rule, Begag's parents were illiterate. At the Ecole Léo-Lagrange, a short walk from Le Chaâba, the young Begag learned to read and write. This unlocked the key to opportunities that had been denied to his parents, paving the way for what was to become a multifaceted career as a sociologist, novelist, screenwriter, and political commentator. When the newly appointed minister

returned to Lyon in 2005, it was to present awards to local children who had won the Savoir Lire [Learning to
Write] prize, awarded by volunteer-staffed associations
working to raise literacy levels. Begag told the young
awardwinners that, when he was a child, one day his father gave him a book: "'This book is a bird,' my father
told me. What he meant was: 'If you want to become a
minister, you must open this book and fly like a bird.'
Each Sunday I went to the flea market with my father to
buy another book, and it's because I took off and flew
that I am here today."[1]

Begag's best-selling autobiographical novel, *Le Gone
du Chaâba*, first published in 1986, tells the story of his
childhood in Lyon. The action is divided mainly between home and school, embodying two vastly different sociocultural spaces. Amid the shacks of Le Chaâba, where the residents have neither running water
nor electricity, the young Begag is raised as an Arab
child, learning an Algerian dialect of Arabic along with
the moral codes of his Muslim parents. At the neighborhood public school he learns to read and write in
French and is given lessons in correct behavior as understood by the majority ethnic French. In negotiat-
ing a path between the different cultural spaces that he
encounters and the racial and ethnic tensions running
between the majority and the minority ethnic popula-
tions, the young Begag experiences a series of confus-
ing, often comic, and sometimes painful situations. The
child's experiences are recounted by his mature alter
ego with an engaging blend of playfulness, verbal in-
vention, and multilayered irony, reflecting the multi-

cultural melting pot that has become an increasingly important part of contemporary French society.

Lyon, the second largest city in France after Paris, is situated at the confluence of the Rhône and Saône rivers. The historic downtown core of the city spans the area where the two rivers run close together in a north-south direction. Most of the city's extensive suburbs lie to the east of the Rhône. They include relatively old, mainly working-class suburbs such as Villeurbanne, just across the Rhône from downtown Lyon, and, further out, low-cost high-rise housing projects built during the 1960s and 1970s in places such as Vaulx-en-Velin and Vénissieux. The main events in *Le Gone du Chaâba* take place in and around Le Châaba, a cluster of shacks thrown up on the Villeurbanne side of the Rhône, between the river and an urban expressway linking the suburban area to downtown Lyon. In the later stages of the narrative, the family moves to the old working-class neighborhood of La Croix-Rousse, built on a steep hillside between the two rivers, close to the historic heart of Lyon.

The story is set in the 1960s. Until then, migration from Algeria to France had been largely temporary and economic in nature. Since the early years of the twentieth century, impoverished Algerian laborers had traveled to France to take temporary unskilled jobs there. After a few years, they would return to their native land, where their families remained. Fathers were often replaced by sons or brothers in a rotation system that ensured that, while there was a more or less ongoing presence of Algerian workers in France, few of them remained there for more than a few years.[2] In the 1950s, this began to change. Migrant workers began to bring in their families. Now, as economic migration grew in response to the labor shortages experienced by France during the postwar economic boom, so too did the number of permanently settled immigrant families from Algeria and the neighboring North African countries of Morocco and Tunisia. Later, amid the economic slowdown resulting from the oil shocks of the 1970s, the French government attempted to reverse migratory flows from North Africa (also known as the Maghreb), brandishing a mixture of carrots and sticks in the hope of repatriating as many North Africans as possible. But it was too late. By now, migrant families had put down roots in France, where growing numbers of children such as the young Begag had been born and educated. With the economic climate even more uncertain south of the Mediterranean compared with France, few Maghrebis could see any reason to return there.

Public awareness of this transition from temporary labor migration to permanent family settlement took place against a backdrop of sharply rising unemployment and economic insecurity. In the early 1980s, this combination of circumstances was successfully exploited for electoral purposes by the extreme right-wing Front National, under the leadership of Jean-Marie Le Pen, who blamed unemployment (and every other ill afflicting the nation) on "immigration," by which he meant the presence of non-Europeans, especially North Africans, in France. Since then, the settlement of minorities originating in the Maghreb and other Third World regions has been a key element in political, social, and cultural debates in France.[3]

Begag was part of the earliest wave of family settlement by Algerian migrants. His father, Bouzid, from the village of El-Ouricia near the city of Sétif, in northeastern Algeria, had first come to France as a construction worker in 1947. In 1954, Bouzid was joined in Lyon by his wife, Messaouda, and four children already born to them in Algeria. In Lyon, they had three more children. These included Azouz, born in 1957. As they were too poor to afford regular housing, like many other immigrant families from Algeria and other African countries, they lived in a *bidonville* (shantytown) thrown up on spare land with makeshift materials and none of the facilities (running water, electricity, sewers, etc.) that most French people took for granted. Begag started to attend school in 1962. *Le Gone du Chaâba* begins a year or two later (the exact chronology is unclear) and ends in the fall of 1968 with the family about to move from La Croix-Rousse to a new housing project in Vaulx-en-Velin, in the eastern suburbs of Lyon. Their move from this old, relatively central area of Lyon to a new housing project in a more outlying suburb was typical of the way in which many immigrant families were re-housed in similar developments during the 1960s and 1970s, producing dense concentrations of minority ethnic groups in socially disadvantaged high-rise neighborhoods that, in the 1980s and 1990s, became stigmatized as *les banlieues*. Until then, the word *banlieues* (lit. "suburbs") had been a generic term for suburban areas as a whole. Today, in popular parlance it has come to denote disadvantaged multiethnic urban spaces that are the French equivalents of "inner-city" areas in Britain and the United States.[4]

The events described in *Le Gone du Chaâba* take place well before these developments in the banlieues. But it should not be forgotten that the narrative was written during the 1980s, at precisely the time that immigration and the new urban geography of France were becoming major issues in public debate. The earliest drafts of *Le Gone du Chaâba* date from 1981. A complete version of the text was submitted in 1983 in a competition for young writers from immigrant backgrounds run by a small publisher in Lyon. The publisher went out of business before a winner could be chosen. Through a friend, Begag contacted the Seuil publishing company in Paris, which eventually published a much-revised version of the manuscript in 1986. By then, immigration was becoming a key talking point not only in French politics but also in the cultural life of the nation. An initially small but growing corpus of novels, films, and music by second-generation Maghrebis was beginning to attract attention. Hungry for new labels, the media started talking about the emergence of a "Beur culture," with which Begag quickly became identified.[5]

Many of those to whom this label was applied, including Begag, had misgivings about it. The word *Beur* had originally been coined in the 1970s by second-generation North Africans in the banlieues of Paris. It is generally considered to be a piece of *verlan* (back slang), formed by inverting and partly truncating the syllables of the word *Arabe*, which was often tainted in

French usage by pejorative connotations inherited from the colonial period. By calling themselves *Beurs* instead of *Arabes*, second-generation North Africans hoped to escape the stigmatizing effects of the latter.[6] The new word first came to the attention of the general public in 1983 in media coverage of a nationwide march organized that year by second-generation North Africans. Officially called the Marche pour l'egalité et contre le racisme [the March for equality and against racism], it was dubbed by the media the Marche des Beurs [the March of the Beurs]. Thereafter, *Beur* rapidly entered general circulation, becoming a recurrent feature in subsequent media coverage of the banlieues. The negative connotations attaching to media representations of the banlieues were one of several reasons why Begag and others tended to become reluctant to be labeled *Beurs*.[7]

Negative perceptions of France's North African minority were an important part of the context in which *Le Gone du Chaâba* was written and published. Although the narrator-protagonist never refers to events later than those of his childhood in the 1960s, he often speaks with a linguistic and perceptual subtlety that can only be that of the adult author. This older figure, who wrote the narrative in the first half of the 1980s, was intensely aware of the animosities whipped up by politicians and others against Maghrebis during this period. But, instead of denouncing misperceptions head-on by writing about the immediately contemporary situation, Begag sought instead to create a better understanding of France's North African minority by returning to an earlier period and presenting it through the often naive eyes of his childhood alter ego. The young protagonist's respect for French authority figures and the frequent self-mockery with which events are narrated gently undermine the claims of those—numerous in the 1980s and still significant in number today—who present France's North African minority as a threat to national identity. Thus, while not directly addressing the tensions and hostilities present in the 1980s, the text serves in many ways as an antidote to them, inviting majority ethnic readers to enjoy the company of engaging and often humorous characters grappling with serious problems that are shown to be best tackled with good rather than ill will.

An important factor that had often poisoned Franco-Algerian relations lay in the colonial period and its legacy. When Begag was born in 1957, Algerian nationalists were in the midst of waging a guerrilla war against French rule, which had first been imposed on Algeria by military conquest beginning in 1830. Echoes of that period and of the bitter struggle through which French rule was eventually ended with Algerian independence in 1962 are dotted through the text. A subtle example lies in the statue of Sergeant Blandan in the Place Sathonay, at the foot of the hill on which the Croix-Rousse neighborhood is located. Although Begag does not mention this in *Le Gone du Chaâba*, the soldier commemorated by the statue, Sergeant Pierre-Hippolyte Blandan, was a native of Lyon who died in Algeria in 1842 at the hands of Arab troops resisting the French conquest. A more explicit reminder of the colonial period is Begag's high school teacher, Monsieur Loubon, a *pied-noir* [white settler] from Algeria. When independence came in 1962, most pieds-noirs fled Algeria and resettled in France. Many were bitter about the end of French rule and the losses they had suffered on leaving Algeria. Smoldering resentment of this kind was one of the factors that would later help fuel support for Jean-Marie Le Pen's Front National. Monsieur Loubon is a notable exception to this pattern. Nostalgic for Algeria, he takes pleasure in linguistic and cultural exchanges with the young Begag, who, at the time of the events described in the narrative, has never set foot in Algeria. In this way, Begag learns from a pied-noir teacher many things about his so-called home country that his illiterate parents have never had the skills to teach him. At the same time, he gently asserts his own linguistic skills by commenting in an aside that, seemingly without knowing it, Monsieur Loubon speaks his brand of Arabic with a Berber accent, Berber being the language spoken in Algerian regions such as Kabylia. Through such exchanges Begag's relationship with Monsieur Loubon typifies his celebration of cultural diversity despite the political and other tensions that have often divided different ethnic groups.

This diversity is deeply embedded in the narrative fabric of *Le Gone du Châaba*, which is peppered with words in Algerian Arabic, Lyonnais slang, and other nonstandard forms of French, including the heavily accented French of Begag's immigrant parents.[8] The text switches frequently—sometimes within the space of a single sentence—not only between different languages (principally French and Arabic) but also between multiple linguistic registers (now formal, now colloquial, mixing baby talk with occasional adult crudities). This kind of linguistic richness is notoriously difficult to translate. In theory one might attempt to render Begag's mixture of French and Arabic slang by some comparable mixture of English and some other slang (e.g., the sociolect of Puerto Ricans in New York or of Pakistanis in London). In practice, such a linguistic transposition, mixing Spanish or Urdu with Bronx or cockney slang, would simply introduce a new set of problems and linguistic complexities to no very useful purpose, and the elimination of the original linguistic mix would drain the text of many of the specificities of Begag's narrative, which cannot be fully understood if they are detached from the particular circumstances that are those of North Africans in France.

In order to convey that specificity the translation retains all the Arabic colloquialisms and many of the French ones, together with instances of nonstandard pronunciation of French where these are featured in the original text. English translations are provided where such terms first appear and/or in glossaries at the end of the book. This too is in keeping with the spirit of the original text, which deliberately mixed nonstandard pieces of French pronunciation with liberal doses of Arabic and Lyonnais slang unfamiliar to the average French reader, for whom only occasional translations or explanations were provided in the main body of the narrative. In this way the reader was encouraged to widen his or her linguistic and cultural horizons by inferring the meaning of unfamiliar terms from their contexts within the flow of the narrative, rather than having his or her attention deflected to external notes or other forms of editorial apparatus. It is noteworthy that Begag's original manuscript contained no translation of the Algerian Arabic colloquialism *chaâba* [a patch of spare land containing roughly improvised dwellings, used as a proper noun to designate the bidonville in which he was brought up]; neither did it furnish an explanation of the Lyonnais slang word *gone* [kid]. These two words, fused together in the title of the novel, symbolized its multicultural dynamic, and their meaning could be grasped by the reader only through immersion in the multiethnic context in which this fusion had occurred.[9]

Prior to publication a set of glossaries was added by the author at the suggestion of his publisher, Seuil, to assist readers who might not otherwise be able to figure out some of the linguistic particularities of the text. Positioned at the end of the book, these glossaries provide a useful and relatively discreet fallback, leaving the flow of the text free to draw the reader into the world of the narrator-protagonist uninterrupted by notes or other external distractions. A similar approach has been adopted in the English translation. Because, compared with Britain or the United States, France has generally had closer cultural relations with the Arab world, a significant number of Arabic terms have entered general usage in France and require little or no explanation there. The number of terms requiring explanation is inevitably larger for English-speaking readers. In recognition of this, translations of foreign locutions are provided more systematically on their first occurrence in the English-language text, and the glossaries have been expanded and adapted (in consultation with the author) to meet the needs of English-speaking readers. Fundamentally, however, in keeping with the original text, the translation endeavors to draw the reader into the world of Begag and his family as nearly as possible on their own terms, rather than transposing them into an Anglophone sociolect or overloading the text with intrusive editorial explanations.

In the twenty years since *Le Gone du Chaâba* was first published, Begag has built a distinguished career as a sociologist, writer, and now government minister. By 2006 he had published around thirty books and countless articles together with numerous media interviews. The key components of his intellectual and political trajectory since the publication of *Le Gone du Chaâba* are reflected in his latest book, *Ethnicity and Equality*.[10] Written in the style of a political essay on the social and ethnic tensions that, in the fall of 2005, exploded in the banlieues in France's worst civil disturbances in almost forty years, the book also displays Begag's trademark propensity for good-humored storytelling in the face of personal and social adversity. For readers who wish to learn more about the thinking of the shantytown kid turned government minister, it offers a richly informative complement to *Le Gone du Chaâba*.

## Notes

1. Sophie Landrin, "Première sortie de ministre pour Azouz Begag à Lyon," *Le Monde*, 14 June 2005.

2. See Neil MacMaster, *Colonial Migrants and Racism: Algerians in France, 1900–62* (Houndmills: Macmillan; New York: St. Martin's, 1997); Alain Gillette and Abdelmalek Sayad, *L'Immigration algérienne en France* (Paris: Entente, 1984); and Emile Temime, *France: Terre d'immigration* (Paris: Gallimard, 1999).

3. See Alec G. Hargreaves, *Immigration, "Race," and Ethnicity in Contemporary France* (London: Routledge, 1995); and Philippe Dewitte, ed., *Immigration et intégration: L'état des savoirs* (Paris: La Découverte, 1999).

4. See Alec G. Hargreaves, "A Deviant Construction: The French Media and the 'Banlieues,'" *New Community* 22, no. 4 (October 1996): 607–18; and "Cities/Banlieues," special issue of *Contemporary French and Francophone Studies*, vol. 8, nos. 1 and 2 (January and April 2004).

5. See Alec G. Hargreaves, *Voices from the North African Immigrant Community in France: Immigration and Identity in Beur Fiction* (Oxford: Berg, 1991; 2nd, expanded ed., Oxford: Berg, 1997); Michel Laronde, *Autour du roman beur: Immigration et identité* (Paris: L'Harmattan, 1993); Alec G. Hargreaves and Mark McKinney, eds., *Post-Colonial Cultures in France* (London: Routledge, 1997); and Hafid Gafaïti, ed., *Cultures transnationales de France: Des "Beurs" aux . . . ?* (Paris: L'Harmattan, 2001).

6. An alternative view is that *Beur* may be a contraction of *Berbères d'Europe* [Berbers of Europe]. Although it is true that many North African migrants to France spoke Berber rather than Arabic, the majority ethnic population was generally unaware of this and tended to label all Maghrebis *Arabes*. Similarly, since its earliest recorded usage, *Beur* has served to denote all second-generation Maghrebis of both Arab and

Berber descent. Granted this generalizing function, it seems more likely that *Beur* was coined as an inversion of *Arabe* rather than as a contraction of *Berbères d'Europe*.

7. Sylvie Durmelat, "Petite Histoire du mot 'beur,'" *French Cultural Studies* 9, no. 2 (June 1998): 191–207.

8. The hybrid nature of the everyday speech of Algerians such as Begag's parents, mixing Arabized French with Arabic dialect far removed from the classical Arabic originating in the Middle East, is reflected in the suggestion of Alek Baylee Toumi that such speech be labeled as *Farabic* (see Alek Baylee Toumi, *Maghreb Divers* [New York: Peter Lang, 2002], 133–38).

9. In an interview, Begag explained: "*Gone* is an idiomatic term used in Lyon to denote a child, similar to *minot* in Marseilles and perhaps *titi* in Paris. *Chaâba* is the name of the shantytown where I lived and grew up until the age of ten or eleven. . . . We lived in temporary, makeshift conditions comparable to those of people living in the *favellas* of Brazil and the *barrios* in other parts of Latin America. It was the inhabitants of *Le Chaâba* who gave it that name as a kind of ironic commentary on their poor living conditions: *Chaâba* is more or less synonymous with *hovel*. . . . Calling our living quarters *Le Chaâba* was a way of saying: 'What a slum!'" ("L'Invité: Azouz Begag" [an interview with Corinne Martin and Thierry Paquot], *Urbanisme*, no. 325 [July–August 2002]: 72). In reading the translation, care should be taken not confuse the Lyonnais slang word *gone* with its English homophone (the past participle of the verb *go*).

10. Azouz Begag, *Ethnicity and Equality: France in the Balance*, translated by Alec G. Hargreaves (Lincoln: University of Nebraska Press, 2007).

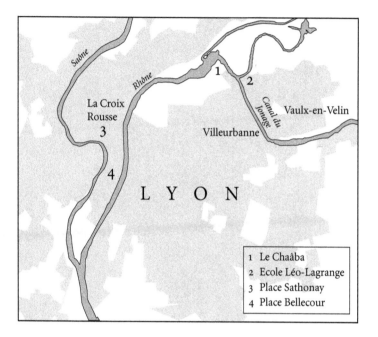

Map of Lyon showing principal locations mentioned in the text.

Azouz Begag with his parents, 1965. *Courtesy Azouz Begag
private collection.*

Azouz Begag, minister for equal opportunities, 2005.
*Courtesy* sppm/*Matignon.*

## Shantytown Kid

*[ Le Gone du Chaâba ]*

Zidouma was doing her morning laundry. She had gotten up early so she could take up position at the only source of water in the shantytown, *l'bomba* [the hand pump], which drew drinking water from the Rhône. In the little redbrick pool that Berthier had designed to hold water for his garden, she wrung out the water, then scrubbed and beat the heavy, sodden sheets on the hard ground.

Bent double, her body at a right angle, as she soaped with her *saboune d'Marsaille* [Marseilles soap], she pulled once, then again at the pump to draw the water. She scrubbed again, rinsed, drew the water, and wrung out the cloth with her two strong arms. She seemed to repeat these motions endlessly. Time passed. She knew full well that there was only one place to draw water here at Le Chaâba, but her manner was very determined. She wanted to take her time, lots of time. And if someone should be bold enough to say anything to her, they would get what they deserved!

That someone was indeed waiting a few yards away. It was Zidouma's neighbor, who lived in the shack right next to hers. She was holding a bucket in which were piled dirty sheets, children's clothes, rags. She waited patiently, patiently. Zidouma, untiring, did not even bother to look around, although she had already felt the presence of someone standing behind her for a couple of minutes, someone showing signs of annoyance. She even started to slow down.

The neighbor still waited patiently, patient . . . no, she lost her patience. Dropping her bucket, she charged forward like a billy goat toward her rival. The collision was terrible. The two women locked in combat, screaming war cries from the depth of their throats.

Attracted by the commotion, the other women came out of their shacks. One of them, belonging to one of the community's two clans, placed herself between the two belligerents to pacify them. Supposedly to calm down the most agitated of the two, she dealt her a terrible backhander on the right cheek. That was all my mother needed to plunge into the fray. Leaving me to my morning coffee, she advanced her ample frame while bellowing insults.

I did not try to stop her. You cannot stop a charging rhinoceros. I finished my beverage hastily so that I could go and watch the fight. I did not know why, but I liked sitting on the steps of our home watching these scenes played out in front of l'bomba and *le baissaine* [the pool containing water from the pump]. It's so curious to see women fighting.

⟨ ⟨ ⟨

Clan against clan, pitted against each other behind the big wheels of Le Chaâba—my mother and my Aunt

Zidouma—the women couldn't resist poisoning each other's lives.

"I hope Allah gouges your eyes out!" cried one.

"I hope your shack burns down tonight, you bitch, and I hope death gets you in your sleep," replied another.

I didn't know women were so resourceful. Even my mother—she wasn't one to be left behind. Each time war broke out between them, they tore into each other, ripping their *binouars* [dresses], and pulling out each other's hair. They flung newly washed sheets and clothes into the mud, spat out the most colorful and expressive insults from the depths of their throats, and hurled curses against each other. I enjoyed this street theater. One day I even saw Zidouma making a funny gesture with her finger while saying to another woman who belonged to my mother's clan: "Here, take this!"

She was thrusting out her right hand, with all the fingers folded except for the middle one, which stood erect at a right angle. Her adversary swore at her like a demon before becoming totally hysterical. She lifted up her dress with her left hand, tilted her body slightly back, then, with the right hand, she pulled down her enormous white undies. Her naked privates, covered by her hand, were thus enlisted as a weapon in the battle of nerves.

I was intrigued by this display. But the performer, catching my curious eye, covered herself up. I blushed without knowing why.

L'bomba was only a pretext. As none of the women

went out to work, from dawn to dusk they were stuck between the corrugated iron roofs and the floorboards of the shantytown. They took little notice of whose turn it was to wash the yard or clean the garden or the toilets. Nerves easily became frayed.

After each altercation the women always wished they could hate each other until the end of their lives, but, inevitably, the light of the following day put out the embers of the previous day's anger. Nothing changed from one day to the next: the shacks were still planted firmly in the same spot; no one moved out. And there was still only one source of water in the oasis.

In Le Chaâba people could not hate each other for more than a few hours. Besides, after the rioting at l'bomba, the women started keeping cans of water permanently in their shacks, where they washed the clothes in a tub.

In the evening, when the men returned from work, not a word was said to them about the incidents that had happened during their absence from Le Chaâba. The women held their tongues for they knew that, though it was difficult living there, they had nothing to gain by setting the men against each other.

( ( (

When you saw Le Chaâba from the top of the embankment that overlooked it or from the large wooden gate at the main entrance, you would have thought it was a lumberyard. Wooden shacks had sprouted up in the garden bordering the original concrete house. The main central alleyway, patched with lumpy concrete, now stood between two enormous stretches of corrugated iron and planks sticking up and out in every direction. At the end of the alleyway the privy hut stood isolated from everything else. The original house, in which I lived, was now hardly distinguishable amid this chaotic mass. The shacks stood together, clinging to each other all around the house. A fierce gust of wind could bring them down in a single blow. This shapeless mass merged seamlessly into the embankments surrounding it.

Bouzid returned from work. As usual he sat on the doorstep, took out a tin of *chemma* from his pocket, put it in the palm of his hand, and opened it. With three fingers he pulled together a little ball of tobacco, kneaded it in his hand for a moment, and, opening his mouth as if he were at the dentist's, squeezed the tobacco between his back teeth and his cheek. He closed his mouth and the tin, then threw an inquiring glance across the huddle of shacks that he had allowed to be thrown up there. How could he have refused hospitality to all those relatives from El-Ouricia fleeing the poverty of Algeria?

〈 〈 〈

The men of Le Chaâba had recently dug a big hole in the garden and placed in it a large empty heating oil drum, open at the top. Over this tank they had built a shelter from planks. The shantytown now had its sanitary installation.

Today the tank had overflowed. Bouzid, perplexed by this nauseating eruption, loudly cursed the clumsy idiots who had dropped their surplus offerings on the wooden boards. It was not the first time that he had noticed such droppings. Noisy green flies as big as sparrows filled the cabin, buzzing. Bouzid and his brother Saïd rolled some rags around their hands, then put handkerchiefs across their noses and mouths and tied them behind their heads. With great difficulty they lifted up the ghastly tank. Their faces stiffened behind the handkerchiefs. Followed by the swarms of flies, they moved toward the embankment to empty the tank into another hole. As they went past, the kids threw stones into the still warm mobile pool of mud. When they returned, they dug a fresh hole in a new corner of the garden. The sparrow-sized flies sat waiting for new offerings.

❬ ❬ ❬

By six o'clock Le Chaâba was already bathed in darkness. In their shacks families had lit their oil lamps. A new night was beginning. My brother Moustaf was lying on my parents' bed engrossed in the cartoon strip adventures of Blek le Roc. My sisters Aïcha, Zohra, and Fatia were busy in the kitchen with my mother. Tonight's menu was peppers grilled on the stove. Smoke had already drifted into all the rooms. I was listening to the hit parade on the radio. I began to feel that it would be good to go to the toilet. But I had to resist. Yes, I had to. Hold your breath! Come on, try! It'll go away. No, it was coming back. Hold on! I had to hold on! Why? I knew that, when it was dark, you shouldn't go to the toilet because it brought bad luck and the *Djnoun* [evil spirits] resided there. My mother said they loved dirty places. So I mustn't go there now. No, it wasn't that I was scared, but you mustn't mess with that sort of thing. I held my tummy tightly with both hands as if to place a tourniquet on it. Too late! The dam was giving way. I looked around me, beseeching with my eyes some understanding soul to accompany me. It was a waste of time. Moustaf would simply tease me as usual. What about the girls? The girls—no, I couldn't ask them to help me with something like this. It wasn't something you could ask of women. Too bad, I was on my own. Panic set into my waterworks. The last flood-gate was about to give way. The torch? Where was the electric torch?

"Zohra! Where's *l'lamba* [the lamp]?" I shouted, my voice trembling.

Forget about the lamp; time is running out. I went outside. In a fraction of a second I covered the distance between the house and the *bitelma* [privy]. My pants were already rolled down over my sandals. I opened the heavy wooden door, which seemed to be falling off its hinges. There was no one there. I concluded that the den was empty.

In almost total darkness I squatted over the tank. My left shoe sank into some clumsily placed droppings. But that didn't worry me. I was feeling calmer. The river could now flow in peace. But I pushed frantically on my stomach to finish the job quickly.

Suddenly a noise louder than all the others that had been making me jump for the last few minutes tore into the nocturnal silence of Le Chaâba. Panic-stricken, I pricked up my ears. The steady noise was getting clearer and louder. Footsteps—yes, these were footsteps. They were coming closer. A shiver crept through me, chilling my bones. The door, which I had not locked so that I could make a quick getaway if the Djnouns attacked me, suddenly opened. Hastening to grasp my pants so as to pull them up, I forgot to utter our ritual call, "There's someone in here!" A shadowy figure made a rapid gesture, and a warm liquid drowned my face, flooding into my mouth. It smelt of pee. It was pee! I uttered a stifled cry. My Uncle Ali had just emptied his chamber pot right in my face! He was as startled as I was but helped me up before I could utter a word. He laughed heartily while I tried to wring out my dripping shirt, then carried me back into the house. Moustaf jumped anxiously out of bed. My mother and my sisters came running in, panic-stricken. Ali reassured them, and they all burst out laughing. With her mouth wide open and her round eyes shining like pearls, my mother gave way, her ample North African body convulsed with laughter. Finally, when she calmed down and her body stopped shaking, she pulled out from behind the stove the large chipped green tub that served as a bathtub for the family. Then she took a hard flannel and scrubbed my body vigorously while Aïcha boiled more water in the kitchen.

Now I knew two things. First, I must never again go to the privy at night. Second, when I needed to, it was better for a man such as me to leave the area of the shacks and find a quiet corner outside. There were plenty of ready-made sites in the vicinity, and, in any case, in Le Chaâba only women used the covered privy. The men hid behind bushes or between two poplar trees. I regularly saw them sneak off deep into the forest with an old can full of water. For us folks in

Le Chaâba, paper was something you kept for lighting the fire.

My mother finished by rubbing me with *eau de colonne* [lavender water] from the bottle in a cupboard she guarded jealously for use solely on special occasions. Well, this was a situation calling for emergency measures. She wrapped me in a blanket, carried me in her arms, and set me down on the big bed next to Moustaf, who was busy reading again. Before she returned to the kitchen, her head suddenly rotated in the direction of the window. She had just heard the deep voice of her husband. It was a signal. Whenever Bouzid came home with a guest without having told his wife in advance, he would speak loudly so that she had enough time to prepare a warm welcome. Messaouda understood the message. She grabbed the tub, still full of dirty water, and slipped it unceremoniously under the bed, then straightened the chairs up against the table while removing her apron and tidying the huge embroidered pillowcases decorating the bed. She prepared to open the door to the two men. I asked her who the guest was that my father was bringing home so late in the evening.

"It's Berthier," she told me. "The previous owner of our house."

❝ ❝ ❝

The two men talked late into the night, reminiscing amid loud laughter about their first meeting at the building company in the rue Grand-Bandit (Garibaldi). I couldn't help hearing all the details of their story and was impressed by the ability of this Frenchman to understand and translate my father's words. My goodness, the night flew by!

《 《 《

Did I wash my face that morning? Did I at least put my pants on? I put my hands on my thighs. Everything was fine; I had not gone out naked. I could continue walking to school with the rest of the *gones* [kids] from Le Chaâba.

What about my father, who had woken up at five o'clock in the morning? Had he been able to find his way to the building site on his moped? Why hadn't he told old Berthier that he still had a job to go to, that he needed his sleep, and that he wanted him to leave?

Oh! The sacred laws of hospitality!

While I was feeling sorry for my poor father, Rabah ran ahead of me.

"Stop! Stop, everyone! I have something to show you."

The convoy stopped.

"Do you know how to kiss a woman?"

The assembled masses, with little experience in the matter, stood speechless, while Moustaf attempted to reply, not very convincingly:

"Yeah, I do. You kiss each other's mouths."

"No, that's not it," replied my cousin. "I'm the only one who knows. D'you want to know?"

No one reacted.

"Don't you want to know? Fine, I won't tell you!"

He took a few more paces ahead and turned round to face us again.

"I'll tell you anyway. Well, you open your mouth,

and you put your tongue in the woman's mouth! That's how you do it!"

There was still no reaction.

"You touch each other's tongues, you see! It's not hard. Like this."

Opening his arms wide as if he were holding a woman, he bent his head to the right, pursed his lips, stuck out his tongue, and started wiggling it about weirdly in all directions.

What a strange thing to do! The French were really quite mad! It was just as well they didn't chew pieces of chemma! Rabah's lesson had frozen everybody on the spot. Sensing that his audience was confused, he approached Saïda so as to undertake a practical demonstration.

"Don't move, Saïda. We're going to show them how French people kiss."

Surprised, then petrified, she turned around and, abandoning her school satchel in a bush, ran like a startled rabbit all the way home. I did not understand what was happening but laughed heartily when I saw Rabah roaring with laughter.

The convoy set off again.

Saïda was far away now, but she turned around, cuffed her hands around her mouth like a loudspeaker, and shouted:

"You swine! I'm going to tell your mom and dad!"

My cousin's laughter redoubled. Everyone laughed with him. My tiredness from the previous night's lack of sleep had almost vanished.

Then Rabah turned to my brother.

"You didn't know how to kiss a girl, did you?"

"No. Who told you?"

"At the market—I found it all out at the market. And it's not the only thing. Why don't you come and work with me on Thursday and Sunday mornings?"

"My dad doesn't want us to work at the market."

"Forget about your dad. I didn't bother asking mine!"

"Yeah, but things are different at my folks."

"Do what you want. But if you want to earn some dough, and learn how to kiss a woman on the mouth with your tongue, you should come."

〈 〈 〈

At the market in Villeurbanne, where he had often gone wandering around recently, Rabah had found work with a stallholder. He set up the stall, loaded and unloaded the car, and, sometimes, helped sell things.

"How much d'ya earn?" Moustaf asked him.

"One franc fifty a morning—without counting the fruit and veg he gives me at the end of the market, the stuff that's rotten, and the stuff he hasn't sold. But it ain't rotten. I take it all home."

Moustaf knew it well enough. How many times had he seen his cousin return to Le Chaâba, his arms laden with fruit and vegetables, doing the rounds of all the shacks, handing out bananas, potatoes, plums, and onions?

"Mom doesn't like it when I give stuff to everyone. She says we oughta keep it all at home, for ourselves. But there's too much, and you have to eat it straight away; otherwise it'll go bad."

Zidouma did not appreciate the excessive generosity of her eldest son. She had already tried to halt this impetuousness, but in vain.

Moustaf said no more. He was deep in thought.

For some days now Rabah's lucrative activities had given rise to new ideas among our mothers. A few francs and some fruit and vegetables, even if they were overripe, were better than having the gones hanging around Le Chaâba all morning.

Back home all my mother could talk about was the market. More than anything else she wanted us all to go and work in the market.

"Aren't you ashamed of yourselves, you lazy good-for-nothings? Look at Rabah: at least he brings home some money and vegetables. What do you bring me, clinging to my apron strings all day? Nothing but *moufissa* [worries]! Oh Allah! Why did you give me such stupid kids?" she wailed all day long.

The idea of selling olives on the days when we were not at school did not fill me with enthusiasm. Besides, my father had forbidden us to work at the market. He said:

"I'd rather you worked at school. I go to the factory to work, I'll break my back if I have to, but I don't want you to become what I am, a poor laborer. If you're short of money, I'll give you some, but I don't want to hear any more talk about the market."

I completely agreed with him.

Before I buried myself under my blanket, Moustaf came to talk to me.

"Tomorrow morning, you're coming with me, and

we'll go to the market with Rabah and his brothers. Mom's right; there's no reason why we shouldn't go to work as well."

"But I don't want to go!"

"You don't want to go! You don't want to go? Are you a baby or something? You're coming with me, and that's final!"

With that last invitation, he returned to his bed. Having decided to hold my ground, I fell asleep straight away.

((  ((  ((

"Come on, get up! It's six o'clock!"

No, it wasn't a nightmare. Moustaf was indeed slapping me hard on the shoulder. He pulled all the bedclothes off me and threw my warm blanket onto the floor. I did not have the strength to resist this torture, and, instead of suffering more assaults, I thought it better to get up without saying a word. I glanced at the alarm clock: it was five to six. It was the first time I had suffered such an indignity. My mother had already prepared for us some café au lait and some couscous, which I poured mechanically into my bowl. There wasn't much time to savor my favorite breakfast.

She was very proud of us and encouraged us, saying:

"This is how it should be, my little ones. Show them that Bouzid's sons are go-getters too."

Fortunately there would be the local fair, the merry-go-rounds, and the cotton candy to savor later. Otherwise I would never have eaten such an early breakfast.

Quarter past six. I had hardly had time to dab some

water on my face before it was time to go. Daylight was just beginning to show. The air was chilly, and it quickly froze my thin, delicate skin. On the boulevard express-way, on the other side of the garden, orange neon lights lit the road for the few passing vehicles.

Thin streaks of light filtered through the planks of some of the shacks. The men were getting ready to go to work.

"What the hell's wrong with you? It's already six twenty," shouted Rabah, who was waiting at our front door with his two brothers.

Even Hacène was there, somehow standing on his feet even though his eyes were shut. He must have had to get out of his bed because his mother had forced him out with her broom, but he was still half asleep.

Our mothers must definitely have been scheming together the previous evening.

"Come on, let's go!" ordered Rabah.

"What about Ali?" asked Moustaf. "He wanted to come too."

"Tough. We're going," Rabah concluded.

Too bad for Ali! He would not be part of our gang of nouveaux riches. The market workers set off.

After skirting along the embankment where the grass and the bushes were still bent under the weight of the morning dew, we entered the Avenue Monin, along which were scattered some regular houses. No light emerged from their closed shutters. Everybody in there was asleep.

Rabah pulled a packet of cigarettes out of his pocket and stuck one between his teeth. I didn't know he smoked. He explained what we had to do when we arrived at the spot to try to get hired.

"You wait till a stallholder arrives with his truck. As soon as he starts to put up his stall, you go up to him and say: 'Please, Monsieur, are you hiring?' It's easy."

"Please, Monsieur, are you hiring?" What a stupid thing to say. I didn't feel brave enough to utter those words.

Quarter to seven. We arrived at the square where the market was held. We walked very quickly to get there before the stallholders, but, even so, some of them had already got their stalls set out. Others were busy putting up their stands.

We all stood together in the middle of the square, our eyes fixed like searchlights on all the approaching vehicles. Rabah noticed his boss, ran to greet him, and came back for a few minutes to encourage us.

"What are you waiting for? You have to go and ask. They're not gonna come looking for you," he said, as if he felt sorry for us.

He grabbed one of his brothers, pushed him by the shoulder, and said:

"Go on, you go and ask the fat guy over there."

His brother did as he was told. We all watched the proceedings, waiting anxiously. It worked. That was one taken care of.

Eventually, all the others found work. I found myself alone in the middle of the square, shivering with cold and anguish. I was ashamed to say, "Please, Monsieur, are you hiring?" The minutes ticked by, and now the stallholders were arriving from all directions, their fruit and vegetable stalls filling the empty spaces in the marketplace like squares on a chessboard.

On the left, I could see Moustaf unloading crates of pears from a 2cv truck. I wanted to cry. With his arms and his eyes, he gestured to me to get on with it. What was I going to do? Return to Le Chaâba for a proper breakfast? No. My mother would not appreciate that.

I approached an old couple, whose backs were bent double under the weight of their boxes. I opened my mouth:

"Please, Monsieur, are you hiring?"

"No, thanks, my little one. There's already two of us, and that's enough." The man replied without turning round.

Abject failure. Red with shame, I turned toward Moustaf to let him know that I did not want to ask for work any more. He refused to accept my resignation and immediately pointed to another stallholder who was unloading his car.

"There, look at him, over there. You can see he's on his own. Go, go on, be brave, for goodness' sake. Otherwise it'll soon be too late. Go on, run! Take a deep breath!"

I edged toward the man who had just arrived. He was late and moving fast and had not seen me. I tried to get within earshot of him and recited the magic phrase. He turned his head toward me for a moment or two, then resumed his task. At last he said:

"It's too late, young man. I've nearly finished setting up for today. Look, I've only got a few boxes left to unload, but come back at midday if you want."

"Midday? ok. Thanks a lot, M'sieur. Thank you very much. I'll be there at midday."

Resigned to this, I ran to announce the terms of my contract to Moustaf, who was now working nonstop. I asked him to let me return home till midday, but he said that it was too far:

"You'll have to stay here and wait till twelve. There's no point going back to Le Chaâba seeing as you've got to come back here."

"Well, in that case I'm going to go for a walk round the market."

With my hands deep in my pockets and my collar rolled up to my chin, I strolled around the stalls under the various covers of which were displayed in organized chaos an impressive variety of fruit and vegetables, which colored the market square in greens and yellows. A bread stall and a toy stall stood next to each other. Close by, the fishmonger presided over the pervasive smells emanating from his means of livelihood. Women were crowding around him. I pulled up my turtleneck to cover my nose against the fish smells and continued on my way, carving a path with difficulty through the shopping bags, carts, and dogs on leashes.

Oh, look, there's sleepyhead Hacène standing behind his stall. His eyes were wide open now. He smiled when he saw me but didn't way a word, no doubt because of his boss. I smiled back at him. A few yards further along I could hear Rabah's voice, louder than all the others.

"Come and buy my plums; they'll make you shapely! Come and buy my plums!"

His boss had told him to shout this strange sentence. I went up to him and told him of my failure.

"But one of them said to come back at twelve."

"Listen. Look over there on my right. Can you see the little old lady who's selling lettuces? Last week she had a young guy with her who's not come back today. Go and try there; she's sure to take you on."

The little old lady was indeed very old, and she had difficulty walking. Even her apron seemed too heavy for her. She agreed to take me on immediately but on one condition:

"I can give you only fifty centimes."

"That's OK, M'dame," I said to her in my gentlest voice, only too happy to find an employer.

One cannot be too fussy in one's first job.

By twelve, which was when the market ended, the poor little lady had sold only half her lettuces. All the same, she did not offer me any to take home. I helped her fold away her stall and put her goods back in the car. When we had finished, she held out to me in the palm of her worn hand three coins, which came to fifty centimes. I could hardly bring myself to take them from her.

I joined Moustaf and the other boys. They teased me all the way home about my fifty centimes from the old lady and her lettuces. But I felt rich, and that was what really mattered.

( ( (

The following Thursday I returned to the market without much enthusiasm. I went back to the fifty-centime old lady and her lettuces, but she didn't increase my wages.

Next time I said no. I said it so strongly that Moustaf thought better of trying to pull me out of bed. He and the other workers left without me while I continued with my sweet dreams.

Eight o'clock. My mother had been moving up and down the room for several minutes with her broom, rags, sponges, and large drums of water. She was muttering. I got up, encouraged by a ray of sunlight that was warming the bedroom floor.

My breakfast was not ready, but I was not complaining. I went to the stove and made myself a lavish repast of couscous and café au lait. My mother jostled around me, pushing her broom between my legs.

"Get out of the way! Why are you always getting under my feet?"

I got the picture. She did not like me giving up my market job. It was better to go and finish my breakfast on the kitchen steps. The weather was nice for it. Breakfast on the sun-drenched terrace before starting a strenuous day of rest wouldn't hurt anyone.

"Go on! Go and eat outside with the goat and the rabbits! At least they're good for something!"

By way of a reply I pulled my fat tongue out of its hiding place and stuck it out at her, pointed, odious, and cheeky, bellowing all the while.

"You spawn of the devil!" she shouted, throwing her dirty floor cloth at me.

"I'll tell *Abboué* [Dad] you said he was a devil when he comes home."

She roared more loudly.

"Oh, Satan won't take you to heaven!"

"Dead right!"

"*Finiane!* [Lazy bum!]"

"Yeah, lazy and proud of it. And the first thing I'm gonna do is tell Abboué that you want to send us all to work at the market."

Then I bleated at her like a goat.

While she resumed her work, terrified by my threat, I left my bowl on the windowsill and went out in the direction of the embankment. I felt good.

I seated myself on a pile of red bricks that customarily served as an anvil and rested my back against the garden wall. My gaze wandered across the vast stretch of woods that separated Le Chaâba from the banks of the Rhône. This was so much better than wasting the morning on a fifty-centime bunch of lettuces.

"Hi, Azouz! You already up?" asked Hacène, one of Rabah's brothers.

"No. I'm still asleep. What about you, didn't you go to the market with your brother?"

"No!"

He wiped his sleeve across his face, trying to staunch a flow of sticky lava dripping from his nose. There. Got it! Having stopped the nasal hemorrhage, he went on:

"Last time, my boss said he didn't need me any more. I think it's because he saw me stealing a box of fruit."

"What d'you want to do? Shall we go into the forest?"

Stepping over the barbed wire, we went deep into the forest amid trees ten times higher than our shacks, with branches even more tangled than our hair, though it should be said that Hacène's head had the look of a *Gaouri* [Frenchman] with his light-colored hair and bluish eyes.

Creepers hung down from the treetops, wrapped themselves around the trunks, and dangled just above the ground, made bumpy by swollen roots.

My fellow explorer bent down, broke off a piece of creeper, and put it into his mouth. From his pocket he pulled out a piece of sandpaper and a match, then lit his stalk and breathed in deep gulps. The tip of the wood glowed.

"Here, take a drag!"

"No, I don't want to."

"Try it at least."

"No, I told you already. Leave me alone with your smoking wood."

We continued on our way, leaving behind us the smell of creeper smoke.

"That wood of yours stinks. Better not smoke it in the cabin."

Nestling comfortably beneath a huge oak tree, the cabin was still there in spite of its frail appearance.

On days when there was no school, I would spend hours there with the other gones. The girls came once to tidy up a bit, but, when they realized that we wanted to play mommas and papas, they refused to lie down on the boxes. Since then we hadn't done much in the cabin apart from chatting for hours on end, but it felt good there.

Back in their own shacks, our parents weren't worried about us when we were in the cabin. So I suggested to Hacène:

"Shall we go get our stuff and spend the day here?"

He agreed, so we walked quickly back to Le Chaâba.

At home my mother was still cleaning. She had forgotten my tongue-in-cheek behavior earlier in the morning. I slipped into the kitchen, but not before first of all cleaning my muddy shoes on the floor mat outside; then I opened the cupboard. I rolled up my lunch snack in a piece of newspaper and stuck it under my belt. As I wasn't very keen on the idea of eating grass and tree roots to gain a more authentic experience, I took three lumps of sugar and plenty of bread.

I joined Hacène at the edge of the forest. His mother, instead of a snack, had given him a slap on the cheek with her five fat fingers, calling him a *bouariane* [good-for-nothing]. I comforted him, saying:

"At lunchtime we can share my lumps of sugar; then we can go hunting. You'll see; we won't starve."

Sitting cross-legged inside the cabin, he chatted while I made arrows out of green wood, at the end of which I fixed nibs I had collected from the inkwells at school.

We were now ready to go hunting, our bows slung across our shoulders.

"Let's eat our snacks first! You never know . . . in case we don't catch anything."

He liked the idea. Each time he sunk his teeth into a sugar lump to break it, he looked like someone gnawing into the carcass of a boar that had just been killed in the wild forest. I followed his example.

A few minutes later, carefully avoiding stepping on dead wood, we slipped between the trees and bushes looking for game.

After a few minutes Hacène started getting impatient.

"There's nothing here. I'm going home."

"No, wait. For a start, you're making too much noise. That's why all the animals have fled."

We still could not see anything that we could eat. No rabbits, no boars, no foxes, no deer, only birds peacefully perched on the trees who must certainly have found our hunting gear ridiculous.

"Look there. A pigeon."

I opened my eyes wide and felt exasperated by the ignorance of my fellow hunter.

"That's not a pigeon; it's a robin. No point killing 'em; they're no good for eating."

We reached a clearing bathed in a ray of sunshine that pierced through the thick tangle of the treetops.

"Right, now let's hide our weapons in this bush and go hunting with a trap."

He looked at me, puzzled by what I was doing. I quickly constructed a rectangle out of four pieces of wood and covered it with a net. I laid the contraption on one of its sides and propped the other end in the air with a piece of wood that I placed on the ground. It was like an open jaw that I could close with the aid of a long string attached to the small piece of wood that held the trap open.

My prison was ready to welcome its first guest.

I scattered some bread crumbs that I had saved in order to attract the birds.

Hiding behind an enormous oak tree a few meters away, with the string in my hand, I waited for a breadloving bird to come along.

Hacène got very excited when he noticed a goldfinch pecking at my bounty. I signaled to him emphatically to contain his enthusiasm. Now the bird was right in the middle of the trap. I pulled the string suddenly: got him! We ran to the trap. Startled, the bird lay motionless. Now we had to open the trap and grab hold of the bird. I made a proposal:

"I'll lift the trap, and you can grab the bird."

"You're joking! We'll do the opposite," he countered.

"You're scared!"

"You too!"

"Forget it. I'll take the bird without your help. But when it's cooked, you'll eat the feathers and the feet, OK?"

He did not answer. My hands were shaking as I lifted the trap, and, in a rustle of leaves that made my whole body shudder, the victim wriggled out of its prison and flew mockingly away into the sky. In a mean voice, I blamed Hacène:

"It's your fault, chicken!"

He countered again:

"You were more chicken than me."

"I've had enough; let's go back home. You're getting on my nerves. And for sure I'm never gonna go hunting with you again."

Hastening my steps to avoid the company of the "chicken," I returned to Le Chaâba with nothing more in my stomach than a piece of sugar and some bits of bread.

As I approached the shacks, I could see signs of a commotion.

Pushing the brambles out of the way, I bent over to edge my way through two lines of barbed wire and came out into the clearing that stood opposite the shantytown. An extraordinary pandemonium reigned over what looked like a battle zone. Kids were running in every direction, some going inside, then coming back out immediately, others clapping their hands and jumping up and down; the youngest were crying in their sisters' arms while some mothers stuck their noses out to try and figure out the cause of all the excitement.

I turned my eyes toward the other side of the embankment and realized what was going on. Blocking the little lane with its huge iron nose, it was coming up very slowly like some gigantic dessert cart: an imposing garbage truck, full to the brim, and overflowing with treasures on all sides.

The signal had been given very early; I had to act quickly. I ran home to put away my bow. As I did so my mother called out:

"Quick! Your brothers are already on the way there."

I had hardly come out of the house when the traveling treasure chest reached the shacks and started down the stony track leading to the Rhône. The kids were running behind it, ready to charge in. The boldest and cleverest were clinging to the sides so they would be the first there when it started unloading at the tip. The youngest tried to imitate them, fell on the ground, got up again, and ran along unsteadily. Others were literally trampled underfoot by the excited mob. Too bad for them: it was every man for himself, and fortunately the truck had to drive slowly.

We got to the banks of the river. The truck backed up and started unloading under our greedy gazes. The last scrap of paper had hardly slipped out of the truck when each one rushed to occupy his patch, a few square feet of garbage that was immediately declared to be private property.

"This is my patch!" proclaimed Rabah, spreading out his arms, his hands wide open as if to make visible the space to which he had laid claim.

"All this is mine!" I chimed in an authoritative voice.

And then we started rummaging through it all. With my sleeves rolled up to my shoulders and my pants turned up practically to my belly button, I started pulling out of the garbage clothes, old pairs of shoes, toys and more toys, bottles, books, comics, half-used exercise books, bits of string, plates and cutlery.

Pulling vigorously at a bicycle tire buried under some boxes, I scratched my hand on the jagged edge of a tin can. A few yards away Rabah saw my wound and called out to me that I would die of the embankment disease if I didn't return home to have it cleaned up and bandaged. I guessed that he simply wanted to claim my patch. So, no way, I refused to budge from my treasure.

Rabah smiled, then burst out laughing when he could see I hadn't been taken in by his game. Like a good sportsman, he handed me a packet of biscuits that he had just extracted from under a heap of old books. It was time for a break. I ate a quick snack on the work site.

At the bottom of the pile of trash Moustaf was rolling in the garbage, pulling somebody's hair. I couldn't see whose. They were fighting. No doubt over an infringement of property rights! Around them the others continued with their search, their eyes fixed on their patch.

One of Rabah's younger brothers, having found all the booty in his patch, started coming up toward mine. I warned him:

"Stop where you are! This is my territory here!"

He gave in. He knew that his family would in any case have plenty of booty. Earlier on, when the arrival of the garbage truck was first announced, Rabah had told all his family so they could mount a profitable expedition.

Those who came on their own would return with little to show.

After a meticulous search, when all the boxes and cans had been emptied of their contents, I decided to return to base camp. To get all the treasures back to my Aladdin's cave, I tied a piece of string to a crate, piled on it all the books, plates, toys, and rags, and dragged it behind me along the bumpy track. The others did the same, and soon we were all marching in a veritable procession of crates and boxes, throwing up behind us a formidable cloud of dust.

While I was getting ready to unload my crate, I saw Old Ma Louise coming toward me. She was wearing her long worn-out boots and was holding in her hand a stick she used for rummaging through garbage. She sounded in a bad mood.

"Has a truck arrived?" she asked.

"Yeah, but it's all finished now. We've been through it all," I said without thinking.

She barked back:

"You swines! You could've told me. Where's Rabah, then?"

"He's back there. He hasn't finished yet."

She walked off abruptly toward the Rhône.

Old Ma Louise lived with her husband in the little concrete house close to the boulevard. She was an old woman, about five feet tall, with a round face that was barely covered by thinning hair that was usually colored with henna.

Her husband was Monsieur Gu. When he was not working, he looked after his garden. Taciturn, bald, self-effacing, always pale, and with protruding eyes, he often seemed perplexed by his wife's eccentric behavior. He and Ma Louise had never been able to have children of their own, but, if all the children they had adopted in Le Chaâba had been theirs, they would have made a fortune in family allowances.

She caught up with Rabah. He was ramming a moped motor into a box that was already overflowing with the oddest assortment of objects. Tapping her boot with her stick, she harangued him:

"I guess you forgot to come and get me? I know, I know: when a truck comes, you are in hurry; you don't have time to let Louise know."

With his tail between his legs, he mumbled a few incoherent words:

"I knew you wanted to come . . . I wanted . . ."

"You wanted ... Monsieur wanted! You really conned me there! You wanted all the goodies for yourself! Admit it! Louise would have taken some of it from you!"

"No, that's not it."

"So why didn't you come and fetch me?"

Rabah bent his head down sheepishly, exasperated by the old lady.

"I hate the way you look away. Look at me when I'm talking to you! Look into my eyes. There!"

Without speaking or looking at her, he tied a string on his box and headed off down the track without turning around. Behind him, Ma Louise stood motionless amid the pile of garbage. Then she cursed him.

"You act like a big shot, Rabah. But you know you'll end up a loser!"

He couldn't care less. The only thing on his mind was the moped motor.

❨ ❨ ❨

The grand old lady of Le Chaâba was outraged by the attitude of her underling. She would get him in the end.

In a determined mood, she returned home, following a few yards behind Rabah.

It was Thursday, and, as she did every Thursday, she invited some of us into her little house. This was the highest reward any of us could imagine! An incomparable delight for the chosen few!

While we scrutinized the riches we had dug up from the garbage disgorged by the truck, Old Ma Louise, with Moustaf at her heels, went through our rows to point out those who were to have the good fortune of entering her palace.

Today I was among them.

She passed behind Rabah, who pretended not to notice. Disdainfully, he marshaled the strength of a buffalo to control his desire to swear at her and continued inspecting his motor.

She had finished. The committee had been formed. We followed our hostess up to the gates of her residence.

"Wait there! I am going to tie up Pollo."

She went into the garden where the huge wolfhound was prowling, an eighty-pound heavyweight in charge of watching over the property of his masters during their absence and keeping company with the pigeons, the doves, the hens, and the rabbits. All these farmyard animals were kept in big cages near the track that led to our shacks.

Pollo instinctively responded to the barely audible whistle of his mistress. He bounded up to her in three majestic strides. She held him tightly to allow us to get through.

On the other side of the wire fencing the wolf lay on its side, his chin on the lawn, and his black eyes fixed on us relentlessly. His sharp teeth made quite a welcoming party.

We walked by the cages to get to the house. Then we entered Aladdin's cave.

Monsieur Gu was already there. Rocking in his chair, he was quietly smoking his pipe and smiled when he saw us enter.

The room was very narrow and dark. A single small window looked out onto the boulevard expressway.

Above the window stood a wooden clock that struck every hour and from which a colorful nightingale emerged to cuckoo forth the time.

Ma Louise seated us around the table in the middle of the room, which was unfortunately too small to accommodate all the forty gones who were dying to visit the castle.

She poured several pints of milk into an enormous pot that she placed on the stove, put a bowl in front of each of us, poured a spoonful of chocolate into the bottom of each bowl, cut some slices of bread, and left the butter and jam where we could reach them.

I waited to see the milk rise in the pan.

Then the great four o'clock feast started. Sweet, thick slices of bread passed between the bowl and my mouth at such a speed that Monsieur Gu looked perplexed. He knew that in our homes there was never any chocolate or jam. There our afternoon menu consisted of bread and sugar lumps.

I savored the bounty silently.

"Have you finished now?" asked Louise.

Our four o'clock snack had been digested.

"Good. You are now all going to clean up the garden with Monsieur Gu, OK?"

"What do we need to do, Louise?" asked Moustaf.

"You need to pick up the dead leaves, pull up the weeds, and rake the soil. Follow Monsieur Gu; he will show you."

All the volunteers stood ready for the task. That was the price you had to pay to have a chance of being among the select few the following Thursday.

Sick! Oh, yes, Rabah was sick with envy when he saw us emerge from the palace, satiated.

Ma Louise had hit her rival right where it hurt; she had humiliated him in front of all the gones. But it should not be thought that Rabah would be content to leave her with the upper hand . . .

《 《 《

For several days, in a little corner of Le Chaâba that he had reserved for his personal belongings, Rabah had been raising half a dozen chicks. They spent the days chirping away in a cardboard box, hopping about on the straw. He thought he was the only one to know the parentage of these creatures, but in fact everyone in Le Chaâba knew.

Having marveled so much at the old dame's flock of hens, he had decided to purloin from her certain means of reproduction, just enough for him to start his own henhouse.

One evening he had cut through the wire fencing leading to the large cage where the hens were kept and took all the eggs on which they were sitting lovingly. He had previously taken great care to pacify Pollo by providing him regularly with pieces of fresh meat, blood-covered bones and chicken legs that the beast could not resist for long. It had taken a few days to neutralize the dog, who eventually recognized Rabah and no longer barked when he approached, instead putting out a slobbery tongue. Entirely confident under the gaze of the dog, Rabah dug a hole through which he sneaked into the henhouse and robbed the hens of their eggs.

Now his poultry farm was doing well, and the gone

continued to maintain close relations with Pollo while old Ma Louise wondered what disease her hens had fallen prey to. As her dog showed no sign of unrest, she automatically excluded the possibility of a burglar.

Yet, when she told Moustaf about the situation, she was puzzled by something.

"It's strange. For some days now, when he sits at my feet on the terrace, Pollo has been constantly looking in the direction of the henhouse. I get the impression that he's trying to show me something."

Moustaf pretended to be surprised. He knew where Louise's eggs and chicks were, but he did not breathe a word about it, out of solidarity with his cousin. Thoroughly intrigued by the obsession of her dog, Louise decided to follow him one day. He led her naturally to the henhouse and stood still opposite the hole through which the chick thief, who regularly tickled his appetite, sneaked in. She immediately understood why her hens had not produced any offspring.

"The filthy swine!" she cried, turning her gaze toward Le Chaâba.

That night the thief, as usual, appeared in front of the hole in the fence, but this time he could not see the dog. Nevertheless, he slipped into the garden, full of confidence. As he was about to put his hand on an egg to place it in his bag, the enormous wolf jumped on him like a giant bat. He placed both his legs on the intruder's chest and was about to tear his face off with his teeth when Old Ma Louise called out:

"Pollo! Stop it!"

The beast froze, like a statue.

As she approached her prey, the old dame became worried by his pallor and his irregular breathing. She took him into her house and gave him a drink. Rabah recovered his spirits and explained everything.

The very next day, the affair was closed, and the hole in the fence was mended. Louise's hens would start producing chicks again. Rabah would keep his, but in the next-door garden he had made himself a weighty enemy. Pollo had certainly had the last word.

⟨ ⟨ ⟨

In the little track between Le Chaâba and the expressway three prostitutes were plying their trade in the shade of the plane trees. They spent whole days there waiting on the sidewalk, dressed in shorts or miniskirts displaying unbelievably long, silk-stockinged legs.

I had already been to watch them two or three times with Hacène and was fascinated by the different shades of colors they wore on their faces. Hacène thought at first that they used those colors so their husbands would not recognize them if they saw them there. I knew that it was really to attract men driving along the boulevard.

"Have you seen all those cigarettes they smoke?" Hacène said to me.

"It's because they have nothing to do all day. They smoke to pass the time."

"Come on, let's get out of here; one of them has seen us."

Bent double, we walked back until they could no longer see us, and we returned to Le Chaâba through the little clump of trees to avoid drawing attention to ourselves. We would feel so ashamed if someone caught us leering at the whores on the boulevard.

At four o'clock Old Ma Louise came out of her garden to name those who were to be invited for tea. This time Rabah was among the chosen few.

While we were devouring the usual sweet delights, Ma Louise suddenly spun around and ran to the window. She threw it open and started to rage. A passerby had dared cast a curious glance into the room as he was walking on the sidewalk of the boulevard, which was scarcely three yards away.

"You've got a nerve, haven't you? Do you expect me to invite you in too and serve you coffee as well!"

Visibly surprised and taken aback, the man went on his way without saying anything.

Old Ma Louise shouted that it was the hookers who were attracting to our neighborhood cars and seedy guys who would loiter with their hands in their pockets and walk through the center of the shantytown while looking constantly around them as if they thought they were being followed.

A couple of days earlier, more girls had come and installed themselves on the banks of the Rhône, at the end of the little track there, and also on another lane leading out of the shantytown, just at the end of the embankment.

We were surrounded by the whores and the species they attracted.

Louise's agitation didn't spoil our appetite. She sat next to Rabah to discuss with him in an adult manner the crisis provoked by these peripatetic females. I exchanged a knowing look with Hacène, though Louise must have thought that we were too young to know about such things.

"We've got to get serious and take care of this," she concluded, to Rabah's approval.

Then we all left the house. On the way out, Rabah exchanged glances with Pollo.

My father was sitting on the ground on a small piece of cardboard, talking to other men. Old Ma Louise walked up to them, shook hands with all of them, and, lighting up a Gauloise, started talking about the hookers.

"We gotta do somethin', M'sieur Begueg. We're not going to let these whores walk all over us."

After checking that the children were far enough away not to hear his words, Bouzid concurred with the Gaouria.

"*Tan a raizou, Louisa. Fou li fire digage di là, zi zalouprix. Li bitaines zi ba bou bour li zafas!* [Y're right, Louisa. We gotta get 'em outta here, the bitches. *Bitaines* (hookers) is no good for kids!]"

The old man was ready to move into action to restore the moral purity of Le Chaâba.

The following Saturday the first expedition against the women of ill repute was launched.

Judging by the number of tire marks left by cars suddenly braking on the boulevard, Saturday must be a busy day for hookers.

Old Ma Louise had asked Bouzid to allow the womenfolk of Le Chaâba to assist her in expelling the devil women who had descended on them. After much hesitation he had finally agreed.

So that afternoon Louise rounded up my mother, Zidouma, and all the other strong women.

Wrapped in their multicolored binouars, the battalion strode boldly along the little track leading to the boulevard, led by the woman wearing the pants. Some of them hid their heads behind a towel to keep their identity secret.

"Company, quick march!"

There were already plenty of cars parked on the sidewalk between the plane trees. Leading the operations, Old Ma Louise was the first to reach the prostitutes. Inside a vehicle a woman's head was moving up and down in a rhythmic movement. One of the women in the assembled company pushed her nose up against the car window, then screamed in horror:

"Oh, my God!"

She turned pale and cursed herself for having set her eyes on the odious sight. Seeing the mob charging toward them, the whores closed ranks to feel more secure. Dame Louise then ordered the horde to stop and, turning to the women of ill repute, started to speak:

"You filthy bitches! You have to stop carrying on your filthy business here! Can't you see that there are lots of kids in this neighborhood? Get the hell out of here right now!"

"Ya. Git outta here, bitaine!" Zidouma pitched in.

The other women nodded in approval.

Startled at first by the delegation that had arrived so threateningly, the women now reacted insolently. One of them, the oldest, came forward and said haughtily:

"Who do you think you are, grandma; d'you think

you're scaring us with your gang of gaudy women? Well, tough shit. You see, all of us here, we just wanna tell you: go to hell! Do you understand? Go to hell! We're staying here, and you're gonna go back to your yard and your mountain goats and take your Arab friends with you, OK? Go away; get outta here!"

Pow! The riposte glued Louise to the ground. The Arab women hadn't understood a word, but they said yes to everything.

"About turn, everyone," ordered the chieftain.

Without further ado, the company quickly retreated back to the shacks. Now they were going to declare war against the bitaines. As she marched along the grand old lady of Le Chaâba drew up a battle plan.

"I'll send the gones to kick their butts. I'll show those bitches who's gonna have to get outta here."

Behind her the line of binouars nodded once more in agreement.

‹ ‹ ‹

Deeply shaken by the hookers' attitude, Ma Louise summoned the gones of Le Chaâba to general mobilization.

At 7:00 P.M. we were all there, all ears as she explained her strategy.

"You must all hide about ten yards away from where they are. When Rabah gives the signal, you can start. At the end you'll run back here."

Her audience was happy with the rules of engagement. While Rabah was officially appointed head of operations, each one of us was given a task and a rank. Fortunately I was not part of the frontline commando unit. My duties simply consisted of making a note of the registration numbers of the cars parked on the sidewalk.

"If you're worried about forgetting them," said Ma Louise, "just write them down on the wall alongside the boulevard."

She thought most of the men who came to see the women were married, and, if they objected to our clean-up campaign, we would tell them that we had taken down their registration numbers.

"We'll telephone your wife, *hallouf* [pig]!"

Ma Louise said this was a dead cert, but I thought to myself that, if I came on a confirmed bachelor, I was going to look pretty dumb.

The commando unit set off. We got as close as possible to the target and hid behind some bushes. Our hands and pockets were full of stones of all shapes and sizes. I stopped a little further back from the frontline troops, though I too was armed: you never could tell.

On the sidewalk the trade in passing pleasure was in full swing. Two prostitutes were working inside the cars, while the males who were waiting their turn sat restlessly in their vehicles.

Well camouflaged, the warriors of Le Chaâba were waiting for the war cry. Suddenly Rabah put two fingers to his lips and whistled. All the kids leaped to their feet at exactly the same moment.

I ducked down. My knees were knocking with fear.

A torrent of pebbles rained down on the cars like hailstones. They slammed into metalwork and smashed the windshields. As the men and the women got out of the cars in various states of undress, they were greeted by a shower of stones and ran off in all directions, their hands around their heads.

The hooker who had acted big with Ma Louise also took to her heels. As she was running away, her purse burst open, and its contents fell onto the road. Three kids rolled onto the ground to scramble over some coins.

Suddenly a tough-looking guy in his forties came up to the assailants, shouting:

"You bunch of dune coons! Do you think I'm going to let you Arabs start laying down the law in our own country?"

He looked toward me, his eyes fixing the exact spot where I had done my best to become Lilliputian in size. What an unlucky break. The guy was getting closer. His face was taut. He had to pick on me!

"Rabah, Rabah, this guy's trying to get me! Help!"

Four warriors rushed up behind him and pelted him with stones. Finally, he ran off.

The battle was over, and the chieftain ordered his troops back to Le Chaâba.

"Off you go, all of you, run."

I was always the first to respond to that kind of order, especially when it meant running away from danger. I ran as fast as I could and was the first to arrive in Le Chaâba. Ma Louise had been watching the battle from her garden. Noting the damage inflicted on the enemy, she rubbed her hands.

"Bravo! Bravo, *les gones*! You all deserve a big café au lait! Come on, follow me, all of you!"

We all pushed our way through her gate, each of us claiming our share of the battle.

I shouted to Hacène, who was standing close to me:

"Did you see the guy who came up to me?"

"No."

"Well, he wanted to get me. I scared him all by myself. I gave the hallouf a crack on the head. He ran off."

"Weren't you scared?"

"Scared? No! He's the one that was scared!"

At that point, Rabah turned toward us, interested in our conversation. I fell silent.

( ( (

Next day, on the way to school, we whiled away the time talking about our combat with the prostitutes.

It was cool at that early hour in the morning when the expedition set off for our daily dose of education.

With my plastic school satchel slung over my disheveled school tunic, striding out in my badly pressed pants with a head of hair that fortunately never required any tidying, I dawdled with the other kids along the Avenue Monin.

When we reached the prefabs there, dozens of other children joined our group. At the end of the avenue we came out onto the boulevard and walked along it in the shade of the plane trees. Along that stretch we often used to find little white rubber rings that were almost transparent and that Rabah enjoyed blowing up in front of us for a laugh.

Then we arrived at a big crossroads where a policeman stood directing the traffic with much whistle-blowing and gesticulating.

Just beyond was Léo-Lagrange, our school. But what anxiety we suffered before getting there! We had to cross a bridge spanning the muddy, choppy waters of the canal. The very sight of that green water terrified me. On windy days, when every bit of metal on the bridge would be clattering, I gripped the safety rail with one hand and clung to Zohra's pinafore with the other. After that difficult crossing there were only about a hundred yards still to go.

It was just before eight o'clock. There were already masses of kids waiting in front of the gates. Little groups started to form. Hacène approached some boys playing marbles and said to one of them:

"I'll bet you my king marble."

The other accepted.

Hacène sat down, his legs spread wide, his back leaning against the school wall. He put his king marble in front of him. The shooters, a couple of yards away, missed. Hacène collected their marbles and stuffed them into his pocket. Others took a try, also in vain! He won about thirty marbles, then announced that he was ending the game.

During that time I had tried ten marbles against a queen marble and lost them all.

A little further away, a player refused to pay his dues, and a scuffle broke out.

A gypsy boy approached us and spoke to Hacène.

"You want to play your king marble?"

"No. This afternoon, if you want!"

The gypsy insisted.

"You scared that you'll lose your big one?"

Hacène looked at him disdainfully. The boy backed off.

We had only five minutes left, so I suggested going to buy some cheap candies from the shop on the other side of the road. On the way I noticed some of my classmates. They were reviewing for the morning poetry test.

As we walked back the school bell rang. All the school bags were picked up off the sidewalk. Moms were kissing their little ones and offering words of encouragement.

The school janitor opened the heavy iron gates and moved aside to let in all the multicolored pinafores. It was like a dam giving way. The tide swept into the different playgrounds, carrying the boys into one and the girls and little ones into the other.

Between eight in the morning and eleven thirty total silence reigned: knowledge was being imbibed.

( ( (

We entered the classroom in rows, two by two. The schoolmaster sat at his desk.

"This morning we will have a lesson in correct behavior," he said, after calling the register and stumbling over all the Arab names.

He started talking about correct behavior, as was his habit every morning since I had moved up to his school. And, as every morning, I blushed as I listened to his words. There was a veritable *oued* [river] separating what he said from what I was used to doing in the street.

I was simply a disgrace where correct behavior was concerned.

A discussion started between the French pupils and the teacher. They all put their hands up to say something, to talk about their experience, to show their moral compliance with today's lesson.

We Arab kids had nothing to say.

With my eyes and ears wide open, I listened to the debate.

I knew that I lived in a shantytown of shacks made of planks of wood and corrugated iron roofs and that it was the poor who lived that way. I had gone several times to Alain's home in the middle of the Avenue Monin, where his family lived in a real house. I could see that it was much nicer than our shacks. And there was so much space. His house alone was as big as the whole of Le Chaâba put together. He had his own room, with a desk and books and a wardrobe for his clothes. At each visit my eyes nearly came out of their sockets with astonishment. I was too ashamed to tell him where I lived. That is why Alain had never been to Le Chaâba. He was not the sort who would enjoy rummaging in the garbage dumped on the embankment, or hanging on to the sides of the garbage truck, or getting involved in extorting money from the hookers and the homos. Besides, did he even know what *homo* meant?

In class the discussion was getting livelier. Pupils were saying words I had never heard before. I felt ashamed. I often used to come out with words straight out of our Chaâba vocabulary when I spoke to the teacher. One day I had even said to him:

"Sir, I swear to you on my mother's life that it's true."

Everybody around me burst out laughing.

I had also realized that there were some words that I knew only in Arabic, such as *kassa* [facecloth].

I was ashamed of my ignorance. For a few months now I had been resolved on changing sides. I did not like being with the poor and the weak pupils in class. I wanted to be among the top of the class alongside the French children.

The teacher was pleased with the debate on cleanliness that he had started that morning. He encouraged the pupils by giving pictures and merits to those who had participated actively in it.

At the end of the morning the bell rang. Half stunned by the noise, I left the classroom in a thoughtful mood. I wanted to prove that I was capable of being like them, indeed, better than them. Even though I lived in Le Chaâba.

The first out waited for the others to return to Le Chaâba. None of us stayed for lunch at the canteen because of hallouf.

I saw our teacher walking toward the school gate while talking to one of the top pupils from our class. I turned my eyes abruptly in the opposite direction for fear they might think I was spying on them.

All the Chaâba kids were there now. We walked back home.

At home, I hastily swallowed a plate of pasta, then went back outside, even though it was only for a few minutes. Hacène joined me, then the others. We played at shooting down bottles with slingshots, finished repairing the pedal on a *braque* [bike], and continued building a shack out of cardboard.

Then, amid the noise of the shattering glass of the bottles, the stones hitting rusty nails, and the shouting, the call to order cut in:

"Monsieur Paul says it's time for school!"

We dropped everything on the spot, plunged our hands into a basin of water to remove the grime, put on our school tunics, and, within a few minutes, the convoy was ready for the second round of the day.

We set off on our journey for the third time.

Before two o'clock, outside the school gate, earlier business resumed. The gypsy boy from the morning came up and again asked Hacène to stake his giant marble.

"So, you gonna to play it?"

Hacène accepted, sat down, played, and lost. The gypsy went and placed his winnings a little farther away under the angry gaze of the loser.

Two o'clock. We were in the classroom again. The afternoon went smoothly. Since this morning's lesson my ideas were now clear in my head. Starting from today I was not going to be the Arab boy in the class any more. I was determined to be on an equal footing with the French kids.

As soon as we had entered the classroom I had sat in the front row, right under the master's nose. The boy who used to sit there did not argue. He went right to the back to sit in my old place, which was now vacant.

The teacher looked at me in surprise. I knew what he was thinking. I was going to show him that I could be among the most obedient, among those who kept their daily notebooks neatest, among those whose hands and nails did not show the slightest sign of dirt, among the most active in the lessons.

"We are all descendants of Vercingétorix!"

"Yes, Sir!"

"Our country, France, has a surface area of . . ."

"Yes, Sir!"

The teacher was always right. If he said we were all descendants of the Gauls, then he was right, and too bad if my folks back home didn't have the same moustaches as theirs.

((( 

That afternoon I made an impression. My hand was raised up pointing skyward for hours on end. Even when the teacher was not asking questions I wanted to reply. I had not yet been rewarded with a picture or a merit, but that would no doubt soon follow.

The five o'clock bell rang. Everyone rushed toward the exit. Some unfortunate pupils usually had to carry on with their studies at school till a quarter past six, and I was one of them. My parents preferred to know that I was at school rather than in the street. I used the time to do the next day's homework. That evening an unusual wave of enthusiasm overwhelmed me. I was convinced that the teacher had begun to understand what I was trying to do. I had done well to sit in the front row.

I usually hated staying on for extra study at school because Le Chaâba was a marvelous place at dusk. With the return of our fathers from work the shantytown sparked back to life.

School was finished now. I ran all the way home like a madman, along the boulevard, then the Avenue Monin, then the track along the embankment, and finally into Le Chaâba as night fell.

The men formed a little circle in the yard. They were chatting, smoking, and savoring the coffee that their wives had carefully brought out to them. That evening my father seemed peaceful, soothed as usual by the Arabic music coming out of the wireless placed on the ground, in the middle of the circle, with its aerial fully extended.

All around the men the kids were bustling, taking care of their tasks. One of the fathers got up to separate two little urchins who were fighting over an empty bottle.

I found Hacène among a group of girls and boys among whom stood Old Ma Louise. She was telling stories. Everyone preferred listening to Louise rather than doing the teacher's homework. With my piece of bread and my two sugar cubes, I too listened to the amazing tales of Dame Louise.

"Zohra, call your brothers, and come in for supper, all of you," my mother called out from her doorstep.

My big sister obeyed reluctantly. She pleaded with us to follow her.

"Otherwise, it's me who's going to get chewed out by Dad!" she said by way of explanation.

Moustaf followed her, and I joined them.

In the middle of the yard there remained only empty chairs and a large plate in which the men had placed their coffee cups. They had no doubt been persuaded to return to their shacks by the strong smell of *chorba*

[soup], which was beginning to pervade Le Chaâba.

That evening my mother had prepared a *galette* [flatbread], which we ate with dates and buttermilk. In a dish that she had covered with a napkin, she had delicately placed some pieces of the galette that were still warm. Handing them to me, she said:

"Here, take these to the Bouchaoui!"

I went out into the yard and immediately bumped into one of Rabah's brothers, who was bringing us a plate of couscous with two pieces of lamb on top. His father was talking to the head of the Bouchaoui family and inviting him to come and share their dinner.

I wandered off along the central alleyway in Le Chaâba, looking inside the shacks, through the curtains. I heard my mother calling me back to order:

"Now, then, d'ya want to go to bed without dinner?"

They had finished the milk and dates. I started eating the couscous that Zidouma had sent.

It was now completely dark. Everything was strangely calm in Le Chaâba. The contrast with daytime struck one's ears. Pale lights were emerging from the shacks. Radio sets played the soft sounds of Arabic music to the homesick who were staying up late. The men and women now had a few hours of "privacy" in their shacks.

On mattresses laid straight on the floor, the children huddled together. As they slept, women dreamed of escape, while the men dreamed of their native land. I was thinking of the holidays, hoping that the next day we would have a composition to write at school.

☾ ☾ ☾

At eight o'clock that Friday morning I again sat in the front row. Everybody in the class now knew that I was not going to move from there any more.

The teacher was giving us a lesson about well-educated children.

"A well-brought-up child says good morning, good evening, and thank you to adults because those are the things that people with good manners say. For example, a well-brought-up child kisses his parents every evening before going to bed."

He looked down toward me as he pronounced those words. Was he making fun of me or what? I had never, up to now, gone through such ceremonies before bedding down in my *guitton* [tent]. I lowered my eyes, hoping that he would not ask me anything. He continued:

"Has anyone ever gone to greet the headmaster and the teachers in the morning while they are waiting in the playground for the bell to ring?"

Not a single hand went up. The pupils looked in all directions. Who would have thought of going to the head to say good morning when they arrived at school?

With the lesson in good manners over, the teacher told us that until eleven thirty we were going to write an essay. Here was the topic: "Write about a day in the country during the holidays." I took a double sheet of exercise paper from my school bag, stuck my pen in the inkpot, and started writing straight away without making a rough plan. My ideas were already well organized in my head. I couldn't tell him about Le Chaâba, but I would pretend it was the countryside there, just as he pictured it.

I wrote about a child who would go fishing with a net, hunt animals with spears, and catch birds with traps . . . No, I struck out the last sentence. He would think I was a savage. The child also knew how to recognize practically all kinds of birds, eggs, reptiles, wild fruits, butterflies, and mushrooms. His mother had taught him how to milk their goat, Bichette. With his buddies he would ride on the goat's back and on the sheep that were tied up in the meadow. In conclusion I wrote that the little boy was happy in the countryside.

Time passed. We had to hand in our work. The teacher went around the desks collecting our papers. Moussaoui hadn't written anything on his sheet. The teacher said nothing.

During the afternoon we wrote other compositions. I was happy. I worked well. When I returned to Le Chaâba in the evening, I ran into the forest, collected the prettiest dead leaves, and picked some of the mushrooms growing on tree trunks. I hid these items in my satchel before joining Hacène and Rabah, who were building a cart with giant wheels along with some other gones.

A squeak of brakes on the gravel suddenly interrupted the sound of hammering. Moustaf appeared from the school lane, yelling at the top of his voice:

"They're back! They're back! They're by the embankment. The hookers are back!"

I ran out to take a look. They were indeed there, about a hundred yards away from the shacks, on our school path. Their customers were there too.

Rabah joined us. Screwing up his eyes, which were full of mischief, he said:

"We mustn't tell Ma Louise that the hookers are back!"

As she was at work, there was no way for her to find out. We would come back later.

"Come on! Back to Le Chaâba, you guys!"

We obeyed, certain that our chieftain had a devilish idea in his head.

( ( (

A little later an unofficial commando unit set off. There were about ten of us in total. We got as close as possible to the hooker and her man while they rocked about in the car. Rabah ordered us to stop and then said to Moustaf:

"You, come with me. But don't make a sound!"

My brother did as he was told. Like two cheetahs, bent double, they moved toward the car with their arms full of iron wire. Then they slowly rolled the trap around the back wheels. Our eyes took in the scene. How daring! With their task accomplished, the heroes returned.

"Has everyone got ammunition?" asked Rabah.

"Then fire at will!" chimed in Moustaf, showing that he too could give orders.

The bombardment began. The driver started the motor and moved off a few yards amid an earsplitting noise. Then the vehicle halted, unable to go any further with its wheels imprisoned in the wire. At that moment I aimed a perfect throw that smashed the back window. I was so surprised that I jumped backward.

"Cease fire!" ordered Rabah.

Terrified, the two enemy personnel got out of the vehicle. They looked at us for a few moments as if they wanted to say something.

The man tried to disentangle the wheels of his car. Then the hooker took a few steps toward us. She stopped a few yards away. Through her wide-open bodice we got a suggestive view of her pink bust. Rabah and Moustaf couldn't keep their eyes off such a divine offering. Meanwhile the rest of us readied more stones in our pockets.

The hooker raised her arms:

"No, wait, I've got a proposal for you," she said to the older ones. "You look like you're in charge. You know, I have gones of my own. As old as you. But they are not mean like you. Why are you always causing trouble? We're not bothering you any more, so let us get on with our work."

Rabah and Moustaf did not breathe a word. They even began to look upset. The hooker opened her purse. We all stepped back, but she reassured us:

"Don't be afraid. Wait a minute . . ."

She opened her purse, took out a five-franc note, and handed it to Rabah.

"See, take this! Now, you're gonna let me get on with my work! OK?"

Without further ado Rabah ordered us to retrace our steps, promising to provide understanding and protection for the hooker. From that day on every time the streetwalkers came to sell their wares near the dune coons' shacks, where the police never set foot, a commando unit collected our taxes. But Rabah and Moustaf alone controlled the finances.

((( ( (

By now, on our morning walks to school, when we got to the end of the Avenue Monin, Rabah had started leaving us to go off somewhere else with his friend Chiche. We didn't know where they went, except that it was in the direction of Villeurbanne. I would have liked to follow them!

One morning, at five to eight, when the school janitor opened the gates, I walked straight into the inner playground area. There, just in front of me, stood the headmaster talking to the teachers, in the boys' playground. The bell was about to summon us to line up in twos. With my satchel on my back and my tunic carefully buttoned up, I went up to them. I choked out the words *good morning* and held out my hand. Nobody took any notice of me. They were discussing very serious things up there. I looked behind me, in case anyone was watching. Fortunately no one had seen anything.

The teacher's eyes looked at me quizzically.

"What on earth are you doing here, young man?"

I did not know what to do.

"But doesn't he remember the lesson he gave us in good manners?"

It was impossible to retreat, so I decided to raise my voice to catch their attention.

"G'morning, M'sieur! G'morning, M'dame!"

This time, they did look at me. I held out my hand again to everyone. The headmaster burst out laughing. The others did the same, taking their cue from him.

I felt ashamed, standing there with my satchel on my back, my clean tunic, and my neat hair. I retreated toward the middle of the playground. There, or anywhere else, it didn't really matter. I didn't care any more. I felt a fool. The bell rang. I joined the other pupils as they lined up. As we were going up the stairs the teacher put his hand on my shoulder:

"You did well. But you only need to say good morning. No need to hold out your hand. Only grown-ups do that. But you did well. You should always be polite like today."

I hardly dared look at him. I was the only one in my class to have demonstrated good manners. But I would never do it again. I would keep out of the way in the future.

I sat at my desk and put my satchel on my lap. As I opened it I saw the leaves and the mushrooms that I had stuffed in there the day before so that I could give them to my teacher. I immediately shut my bag:

"I won't give him anything; it serves him right."

The morning passed very quickly. I cannot recall at all what the teacher said during the lesson. My mind was elsewhere. The next day was Saturday; I would go to the market with Moustaf.

❨ ❨ ❨

Moustaf woke me up early as usual so we could go to work at the market. The old lady with her lettuces and fifty centimes was now a distant memory. Now we were working for ourselves. We sold wildflowers at the Croix-Luizet market. Lilies of the valley, lilacs, red poppies, mistletoe, holly—anything that could bring in a few francs.

"Come and buy my lilacs. One franc a bunch, three bunches for two francs. Come and buy my beautiful lilacs!"

That morning, all on my own, I was selling flowers in the middle of the fruit and vegetable stallholders. Moustaf had positioned himself a little further away. He wasn't shouting anything, but he made me shout to attract customers. Rabah and his brothers were there too, this time in competition with us.

Working in the market was not really my strong point, but, with the lilacs, we earned a lot of money, at least thirty francs a morning. Moustaf let me keep a few coins. He gave the rest to our mother.

"Let me have two bunches!" said an old lady who had suddenly stopped in front of me.

I bent down to pick up some of the flowers from the ground. Then she ran her fingers through my hair, played with one of my curls, and congratulated me:

"What lovely hair you have!"

I didn't know what to make of her smile. With her flowers in her hand, she continued on her way, turning round to look back every few yards.

"Give me two bunches, please!"

"Yes, M'sieur! Which ones do you want?"

I picked out two bunches at random and handed them to the man, looking straight at him, but still reeling from the shock of the old lady's compliment. Suddenly my stretched-out arm, holding the two bunches of flowers, went limp under the blow of a second shock. Monsieur Grand, my schoolmaster, was standing right there in front of me. I felt weak. He took the bunches, smiling. Turning bright red with shame, I lowered my eyes and made myself look as small as possible in my oversized velvet pants.

The teacher could see what I was going through.

"Hello, Azouz! How much do I owe you?"

What should I do? Run away, perhaps? No, he would think I was mad. I had frozen from head to toe and was incapable of saying a single word. He took my hand, placed three one-franc coins in it and gave me back the bunches of lilacs, then disappeared into the market. I must have lost at least twenty of the forty pounds I weighed! When he had disappeared behind some stalls, I ran up to Moustaf.

"I'm going. I'm not doing this any more. I'm going back to Le Chaâba," I said.

"You gone crazy or something? Get back to work!"

"No, I'm going!"

And I ran off home, abandoning my flowers in the market.

What was I going to do on Monday when I met my teacher again at school? What should I say to him? Would he talk about what he had seen in front of all the pupils in the class? The shame of it! I was convinced that fate had played a mean trick on me. If you sell in the market flowers that you have picked for nothing in the forest, is that behaving correctly? No. If you have been brought up well, you don't do things like that. There were no French boys selling lilacs in the market, only us, the Arab kids from Le Chaâba.

I spent the afternoon in torment and was oblivious of Sunday slipping by.

On Monday morning, after a terrible night, I saw Monsieur Grand again, after carefully avoiding the headmaster and his colleagues. Before entering the classroom he whispered a few kind words in my ear, to put me at ease. Now I knew that he had felt sorry for me. He must have said to himself: "This young foreigner has to work in the market to help his parents make ends meet! What poverty, and what courage!" I was very happy, realizing that I had scored some points and not, as I had thought, lost everything. I wanted to reassure my teacher and tell him: "Stop crying, Monsieur Grand; I'm not selling flowers in the market to earn a living, but simply to stop my mother from nagging. In any case it makes me laugh when I see French people spending their money to buy flowers that nature offers for free." But I was careful not to change the image that the teacher now had of me: a brave boy, full of goodwill. In a word, a child who knows how to behave correctly.

( ( (

I did well in my compositions. At home, in the evening, I resisted the temptation to go and play with the others and did my homework instead. Zohra helped me read, do arithmetic, and recite poems. My father supervised us from a distance.

One evening, as I was walking toward the way out of school, my satchel swinging, I was already savoring the joys of success. What a pleasure it was to know everything at the tip of one's fingers and to answer questions zealously. Around me the other pupils were talking about the compositions. A few yards ahead Moussaoui was walking with the other Arab boys, those who sat at the back of the class.

An Arab lady came in through the main entrance. She was coming in my direction. Her clothing drew people's attention. She was dressed like my mother when she was doing the cooking: wrapped in an orange binouar, with flip-flops on her feet, and a red scarf tied around her head. A woolen belt was tied around her ample stomach. She came toward me, looked at me, and smiled. After greeting me in Arabic she spoke to me in a soft voice as if she was afraid someone might hear us.

"Are you the son of Bouzid from El-Ouricia? Are you the one who lives in the shacks near the prefabs? Listen! I come from El-Ouricia too. I know your family quite well. Be sure to say hello to your mother from me. Tell her: 'Djamila says hello.' I hear you work hard at school. Listen, do me a favor: can you sit next to my son Nasser and help him with his compositions?"

I began to understand why she had come to see me.

"We're all Arabs, aren't we? Why don't you help each other? You help Nasser, and Nasser will help you."

I knew Nasser. He was not very bright in class. But what could I do? What could I say to this woman? I said nothing, not because I thought it was the best thing to do, but because my mind had simply gone blank when faced with this strange request. I felt sorry for the lady. I could understand she wanted her son to be a scholar too, like the French boys. She was still there, standing right in front of me, looking more and more embarrassed. She was begging me in the name of her son, in the name of our shared origins, our families, and all the Arabs in the world.

No, it was too dangerous. I had to tell her frankly.

"I'll ask the teacher if your son can sit next to me for the compositions."

Thinking that was I naive and that I hadn't understood what she was trying to get me involved in, she said:

"You don't need to ask the teacher."

"Do you want me to cheat, then?"

"Oh, you're using big words. I just want you to help my son, not . . ."

I interrupted her.

"If you don't want me to ask the teacher, then I refuse!"

I walked off toward the way out while she continued mumbling. I could hear her cursing me behind my back, but I did not take any notice. Who did she take me for? Now that I was in the teacher's good books, did she think I was going to cheat in the compositions? How naive of her! What about good behavior, then? During compositions I always tried very hard not to tell others what I knew. I was always worried that others might copy my work and steal what I knew, what I had stored in my memory after so much hard work. This poor lady thought that it could be done just like that, that you could sit next to each other and pool your knowledge and then we would both come out top of the class! She really was too naive. There was nothing to prevent her son from working like I did. So why did he not do it? No, madame, you don't understand.

As I went through the school gates, I passed Nasser. He was waiting for his mother. Did he know what was going on? Maybe he didn't know? He said good-bye to me, suggesting that he was unaware of his mother's dealings.

On the way back home, somewhat uneasily but without letting it show, I asked Zohra:

"Did you see Nasser Bouaffia's mother, when she was talking to me earlier?"

"Yeah," she replied. "What did she want from you?"

"She wanted me to help Nasser write his compositions!"

"Oh? And what did you tell her?"

"I said no, of course! Was I supposed to say yes?"

"No. You did well," she concluded, not convincingly.

"You're only saying that to make me feel better."

"No," she said, "it doesn't matter."

"Yes, it does. Tell me!"

"What do you want me to tell you?"

"Tell me what you think!"

"Well, it's true, you could've helped him a bit."

"Help him do what?"

"To review, for example. Or to do calculations."

I hesitated for a moment, confused by my sister's arguments.

"Yes, but that wasn't what she was asking me to do. She wanted me to cheat in the compositions."

"Oh, no, not that. In that case, then, you did really well to refuse!"

My worries about being a poor "brother" were now laid to rest, and we continued on our way.

We arrived at Le Chaâba. I ran straight to my mother to see if she did indeed know Nasser's mom.

"*Yemma* [Mom], do you know Madame Bouaffia?"

"Yes, of course. Her son Nasser is in your class; she told me so last time I saw her."

"Do you know her well?"

"Very well. We've known each other ever since El-Ouricia."

Now I felt ashamed. Perhaps I could have offered to help outside the classroom. I could have gone to Nasser's home to help him with his homework.

"Why did you ask me that?" she added.

"I met her when I was coming out of school just now. She asked me to say hello to you," I said, to put an end to the conversation.

Yemma returned to her washing. I quickly prepared an afternoon snack and went out into the yard, where the usual commotion around the pump and the pool was in full swing.

Zidouma's muffled voice echoed against the front of the shacks.

"Where is Hacène?" I asked her.

"In the shack, I think," she shouted. "Do you think I keep a watch on him to see where he goes?"

I did not respond to her provocation. Then she added:

"Go and look at home if you want."

I approached their den and pulled the curtain that covered the entrance when the door opened and I saw Hacène. He was lying on his stomach in a corner of the room with his exercise books wide open in front of him. Three of his little brothers were crawling around the table with comforters in their mouths. When they bumped against him, Hacène pushed them mechanically away with his arm, without looking up from his books.

Zidouma returned to her den with a bucket of water in each hand. As she strode over her son, she spilled a few drops on him and his papers. Seemingly unconcerned, he wiped the wet paper with his right sleeve.

I walked toward him and kissed his father, who was listening to the radio by the window.

"What are you doing, Hacène?" I said to him, somewhat embarrassed by the atmosphere in the shack.

"Tomorrow our class compositions start, so I'm trying to review, but I can't because of the noise."

Once again, he pushed away one of his little brothers who kept trying to pull a geography book toward him. Hacène made an abrupt movement, and the baby, on all fours, suddenly started brawling loudly as if he had been branded with red-hot pincers.

Zidouma turned around and shouted:

"You're beginning to get on my nerves, with all your papers around the house. Can't you work at school instead of getting under my feet?"

"We have compositions tomorrow," said Hacène, in French.

Then his father, who had remained silent until now, pitched in:

"Go away, get out. I can't hear anything on the radio now because of you. Go and play with your books outside."

The chief had spoken. Now he would have to go and play outside.

"Come on, let's go," Hacène said to me, cursing his parents with his eyes.

Then, as we sat down on the steps in the yard, he remarked:

"After all that, when I bring home my report and I'm bottom of the class, they hit me . . . It serves them right."

"Forget it," I said, trying to encourage him. "Here, do you want me to test you on your geography lesson?"

"Yeah," he said. "I can never learn it by heart. I don't like geography."

"You have to learn it, though," I said.

⟨ ⟨ ⟨

Monday morning. This was the day Monsieur Grand was due to return our compositions and give us our grades.

"You nervous?" asked Zohra, while we were waiting for the bell to ring.

"No," I said to her. "I'm not worried at all because I know I got my compositions right. Last Friday the teacher said he was pleased with my work."

"Hey, hey, Dad's going to be pleased about that!" said Zohra.

The janitor opened the school gates, and we swarmed into the playground.

"See you at eleven thirty," my sister shouted.

"I'll be waiting for you," I said.

A few yards ahead of me, I saw Jean-Marc Laville. Monsieur Grand was always giving him merits to reward him for his good work. He too saw me and stopped to wait for me.

"Hello, Azouz!" he said, holding out his hand.

I returned his greeting. Then he said:

"Isn't the teacher due to give us our compositions back today?"

"You know he is."

"Yes," he said, surprised by my reply. Then he confided:

"I'm really scared."

"Why?"

He looked me straight in the eyes, puzzled by my response.

"Aren't you scared too?"

"No," I said. "As far as I'm concerned it all went OK. Why should I be scared?"

Instead of replying, he suddenly changed the conversation:

"Did you watch TV yesterday?"

"No, we don't have a TV at home yet."

Jean-Marc seemed astonished. He repeated:

"You don't have a TV?"

"No. We don't even have electricity at home."

At that moment my attention was drawn by an unusual commotion near the entrance to the school toilets. I left my companion and went over toward Nasser Bouaffia, whom I recognized among a group of sixth-grade pupils.

"What's going on?"

He stared at me then shouted:

"Look, I'm not talking to you, and you don't talk to me, got it?"

"What did I do?" I said, looking into the toilets where at least ten boys seemed to be shaking with laughter.

Nasser said nothing, so I went into the lavatories to find out what was going on. Rabah was there, with a Gauloise stuck between his lips like all the other sixth-grade boys. I asked him:

"What's going on?"

"Look!" he said, pointing to the top of one of the stalls.

Moussaoui was perched on the top with his head looking directly down into the neighboring toilets.

"It's Madame Bédrin, one of the girls' teachers; she's having a pee," explained Rabah, shaking with laughter.

Moussaoui turned toward us, waved his hand to indicate the marvels of the sights he was seeing, then got down.

"I saw everything," he declared. "She's wearing pink lacy undies."

"My turn!" said Rabah.

Cat-like, he climbed up to the observation post. His legs were dangling down the toilet doors. Then Moussaoui went to the washbasin, ran some water into the palms of his hands, and threw it up at Rabah just above the spot where Madame Bédrin was sitting. Everything happened very quickly after that. Realizing the seriousness of the situation, I ran toward the exit behind Moussaoui, who was roaring with laughter. Rabah slid down to the ground, and we heard the teacher with the pink undies cry out: "You pig!"

Fortunately the teachers and the head had their backs turned when we ran out into the playground. A moment later Monsieur Grand was calling the class to line up in twos. I looked toward the toilets and saw Old Mother Bédrin pulling Rabah by the ear while shouting:

"You're mad! You insolent boy!"

Behind me Moussaoui was collapsing with laughter.

"I was the only one to see her undies!" he boasted to his followers.

Calm was restored among the lined-up pupils, and we entered the classroom. As he passed in front of the teacher's desk, Jean-Marc Laville made a point of displaying one of his most charming smiles. But his lips were tensed up with fear. Going past him to get to his desk at the back of the classroom, Moussaoui put his hand on his behind and swore at him under his breath:

"Faggot!"

He did not respond. It was not the first time that Moussaoui had threatened him. He had already stolen his afternoon snack, his pocket money, and even some of his books. But Laville had never let on about any of this to anybody.

"Come on," the teacher urged us. "Sit down, quickly! I am going to start by returning your compositions and giving you your class positions; then we will finish the geography lesson we started last time."

While a ripple of anxiety ran through the class, Monsieur Grand sat behind a pile of graded compositions he had placed on his desk, next to the school reports that our parents would have to sign. I started getting butterflies in my stomach. I was thinking of the moment when Monsieur Grand was going to say: "Pupil X, first; Pupil Y, second." Or perhaps he would give the position in the class, then the name of the lucky pupil?

First: Azouz Begag? No. That was just an example of how it would work. Everybody knew that Laville was going to come out top. So let's start again. He would say: "First: Laville." And then? Second? Like all those who held hopes, my eyes would be fixed on the teacher's lips in the hope of seeing my name come out of his mouth before it reached my ears. If I weren't second, I would have to wait for the next names. I tried not to think about the agonies of this torture.

Some pupils were showing signs of impatience. The teacher got up, walked toward the middle of the central aisle, with a pile of reports in his hand, and called out the verdict:

"First . . ."

The class braced itself:

". . . Ahmed Moussaoui." Amazement. Horror. Injustice. Suddenly there was not a sound or a movement in the class. Nobody looked at the person in question. Moussaoui, first in the class! It was impossible! He probably did not even know the answer to one plus one. He did not know how to read or write. So how could he have? . . .

Laville's face lost its shine. He had been sure he would be first, and there he was beaten by a boy whose laziness knew no bounds, a boy who was not even French. Monsieur Grand's face was impassive. His eyes were riveted on the paper he held in his hands. He opened his mouth again:

"Second: Nasser Bouaffia."

This time it was me who nearly keeled over. The teacher must be reading his papers back to front, maybe in Arabic. I turned my head toward Nasser. His eyes, wide open, were staring into the void: he was trying to discern, in each of our faces, a sign, the proof of some sort of conspiracy against him, but no answer reached him. Perhaps a miracle had happened. I turned toward Moussaoui. You could see the skepticism on his face.

Laville's disarray became increasingly apparent as each moment passed. Then Monsieur Grand looked mischievously toward us. That was it! Now I knew what he was doing. As he carried on announcing the positions, some pupils started smiling.

". . . Francis Rondet: two before last. Azouz Begag: one before last. And last of all: Jean-Marc Laville."

Now everybody was laughing heartily in the class, including Monsieur Grand, who started handing out the exercise books containing our compositions. He walked up to Moussaoui and told him disdainfully:

"Hopeless!"

The lout nodded in agreement as if to say: "Your grades, you know where to stuff them!"

Then to Nasser:

"Hopeless!"

The boy whose mother had tried to bribe me grabbed hold of his report, then started crying.

"It's too late to cry now. You should have worked before."

He finally came up to me, and his face brightened up:

"I am very pleased with your work. Carry on like this, and all will be well."

Only Laville was left:

"Congratulations, Jean-Marc. Your work is excellent."

I grabbed my report with both hands and with such an intense emotion that I felt like screaming and kissing the teacher as I thought of the pride my father would feel when he heard the news. The teacher had written in one column "second out of twenty-seven" and in another "very good work; intelligent and hardworking pupil." I did not know what to say, what to do, whom to look at. And there, in the front row, Laville was ecstatic too, his eyes hypnotized by the number one.

"Starting from tomorrow," Monsieur Grand suggested, "you will sit next to Jean-Marc Laville."

"Yes, Sir," I said, without needing to ask why.

Laville turned toward me, smiling as a laureate would smile at his protégé. I played along with him. Then Monsieur Grand resumed his geography lesson.

⟨ ⟨ ⟨

"You're clever, you are," said Hacène when I told him about my achievement. "I came just one before last."

"Well done!" said Zohra and Staf with an encouraging tap on my shoulder.

We returned to Le Chaâba. Poor Hacène was trailing behind the group. I waited for him so we could walk together.

"Don't cry," I said.

"Yeah," he said moaning, "when I get back home, it's me who's going to get a big walloping, not you."

"If you cry, your eyes are going to look red. If your eyes are red, your father will know that your work hasn't been good, so stop crying."

"Let him beat me then," he cried. "I don't care."

"Don't say that. Wait. We'll call in Zohra. She'll take care of it."

It was indeed on my sister that the fate of each pupil from Le Chaâba rested. It was she who translated the teachers' reports into Arabic. This evening, for example, she would go from one shack to the next, read out the grades of each pupil, trying to mitigate the punishment that would befall the hopeless cases, and showing the fathers the spot where they should put a cross on the report to show they had seen it.

She reassured Hacène:

"Don't worry. I'll tell your father that you worked well this month."

Then she put her arm around his neck and comforted him again:

"Don't cry, come on."

My cousin became a little calmer.

☾ ☾ ☾

Operation camouflage failed miserably. Zohra did go to Saïd's home to comment on Hacène's school results and even said that his work had been satisfactory, but his father, who happened to be a butcher, knew how to read numbers and count. And that was something that my sister had forgotten.

Saïd put his finger on a zero that the schoolmaster had circled in red and asked Zohra:

"What's this zero here?"

She told us that she did not know how to answer at first but had then said it was a zero for behavior, which did not matter. But Saïd did not believe her because of her hesitation. She then returned home, leaving the unfortunate Hacène to his fate.

❨ ❨ ❨

On the way to school the next morning our cousin told us about the tormented night he had spent.

"First he beat me with his belt; then he tied my hands behind my back, and I spent all night like that, on the floor. I slept next to the oil stove."

We all uttered cries of horror, and Zohra blamed herself for not having accomplished her task properly.

"I don't care now," Hacène continued, "because he tore up my exercise book and threw it in the fire."

"He burned it!" I said, completely horrified by this tragic turn of events. "And what are you going to tell the teacher?"

"I'll say I've lost it."

"No," my sister interjected. "I'll go and see him and explain everything. That way, you won't have to lie."

"Yeah, yeah. I don't care, I don't care," concluded our cousin.

There was no point insisting further. School was over for him. Deep inside me, I suddenly had the impression that, if Hacène could not succeed, it was because nature had decided thus, that he would never be intelligent. But me, I was second! I felt full of joy at the thought of having been chosen by fate. Though I tried to push the idea aside, it kept coming back to me.

When we arrived outside the school, all the pupils were already milling around noisily in the playground.

"Hurry up!" cried Zohra. "Everybody has already gone in!"

We hurried our footsteps, and, just as I was going through the entrance gate, Jean-Marc sprang up in front of me as if he had been waiting for me all night.

"Hi!" he said.

"Hi! What's up?" I said, surprised.

"I thought that you weren't going to come today. You know we have to sit together in class?"

"Yeah, I know," I said coldly.

I looked at him again. He added, smiling falsely:

"I didn't want to be on my own."

He needed me, though he was the first in the class. The pleasure that I had felt a few minutes earlier in the face of Hacène made my heart flutter even more. I was going to say something to him (I don't know what) when I noticed Moussaoui, Nasser, and two other Algerian boys from my class walking toward us.

"You, get out of here!" Moussaoui ordered Jean-Marc, lunging a kick at his school satchel.

Terrified, the child genius tiptoed away.

"So?" said Moussaoui with a malicious stare that was full of reproach.

"So what?" I said, having not the slightest idea what he might be holding against me.

With eyes like rocket launchers, he let out disdainfully:

"You're not an Arab!"

Instantly, and without even understanding what I was saying, I retorted:

"Of course, I'm an Arab!"

"No, you're not an Arab, I'm telling you!"

"Yes, I am an Arab!"

"I'm telling ya, you're not like us!"

At that point I was unable to utter a single word more. The last word remained stuck between my teeth. It was true that I was not like them. Seeing my hesitation, Moussaoui went on:

"Aha!, Aha! Aha! You had your laugh when the teacher said 'First: Ahmed Moussaoui. Second: Nasser Bouaffia.'"

"No, I didn't laugh."

"Yes, you did. I'm telling ya."

"OK, fine, if you say so. I did!"

"So you're an idiot. That's what we wanted to tell you."

A terrible feeling of emptiness came over me. My heart was thumping heavily in my chest. I stood there, frozen in front of them, and a thousand different expressions fought across my face. For a moment I felt like crying, then like smiling, resisting, breaking down, begging, or throwing insults.

Nasser interjected:

"And, besides, you won't even let us copy from you."

Another of them added:

"And besides, you're a brownnose. Aren't you fed up with bringing dead leaves and all that crap to the teacher?"

He added:

"And, at break, why are you always with the French kids?"

Everything he said seemed obvious. I felt ashamed. I was scared. I could not answer back because I thought they were right.

In the distance, at the edge of the playground, the pupils were beginning to line up in twos, opposite the teachers. I watched them without moving. The bell must have rung already. I had not heard it.

Moussaoui looked me right in the eye:

"I don't want to fight with you," he said, "because you're Algerian. But you have to decide whether you're with them or with us! You have to make your mind up."

"Come on, let's go in!" shouted Nasser. "The bell's gone."

And they walked away toward Monsieur Grand.

( ( (

Reluctantly, on entering the classroom, I went and sat next to Jean-Marc Laville. I would have really liked to show Moussaoui and my other cousins that I did not want to do it but that it was impossible because it was the teacher who had suggested it and if I wanted to be first in the class one day I had to do it.

They all looked at me contemptuously when they went to sit at the back of the class, as if they had expected me to defy the teacher's authority that morning.

Jean-Marc tried to speak to me. I think he was asking me whether I wanted to sit on the right or the left of our joint desk, and I told him to be quiet because

Monsieur Grand was speaking. To tell the truth, I didn't want my cousins to see me talking to him.

Everybody was now seated. The teacher got up from his desk and began to speak.

"Today we will have a lesson on hygiene," he said.

And he talked for a few minutes about cleanliness, asking questions such as: Is it important to be clean? How many times a day should you wash? The French pupils answered enthusiastically because they had learned all about these things at home. They talked about bathtubs, washbasins, and even toothbrushes and toothpaste. If folks in Le Chaâba had been told that the rules of cleanliness needed so much attention, they would have laughed out loud.

To wash their teeth the adults in Le Chaâba would take a glass of water, hold the liquid in their mouths, tighten their jaws to swish it between their teeth, rub their front teeth with their finger in order to clean the surface, swirl the water around their mouths again, and finally spit out the dirty water. Afterward you would hear them clearing the back of their throats to extract the impurities of the previous day, which they would spit out onto the asphalt outside. Then they would wipe their feet across this substance so as not to disgust the neighbors. And that was that. No need for toothbrushes or Colgate.

"What does one need to wash properly?" asked the teacher again.

Three pupils put their hands up.

"M'sieur, M'sieur!" They chirped up like newborn chicks in a bird's nest.

Monsieur Grand waited for a moment to give others a chance to put their hands up; then he reformulated his question:

"What do you use to wash every morning?"

"M'sieur, M'sieur!" The keen ones continued hissing.

"Jean-Marc," said the teacher, pointing to him.

He stood up:

"A towel and soap!"

"Good. Anything else?"

"Shampoo," said another.

"Yes. What else?"

An idea sprang into my head. Instinctively I put my hand up very high, ignoring the reproaches thrown at me by my cousins a few minutes earlier.

"Azouz!" said Monsieur Grand, inviting me to speak.

"M'sieur, you also need a *chritte* and a *kaissa*!"

"A what?!" he said, with his eyes wide open in surprise.

"A chritte and a kaissa," I said, in a voice that was three times softer than earlier, sensing that something was going wrong.

"But what is that?" said the teacher, amused.

"It's something you put on your hand to wash with."

"A washcloth?"

"Don't know, Sir."

"What is it like?"

I explained to him.

"That's what it is," he said. "It's a washcloth. And you call it *kaissa* at home, do you?"

"Yes, Sir. But we use it only when we go to the showers with my mother."

"And what's a chritte, then?"

"Well, Sir, it's like lots of bits of string that are tangled together, and it scratches a lot. When my mother scrubs me with it, my skin goes really red."

"It's called a loofah," he concluded, smiling.

I blushed a little, but he spoke encouragingly.

"Well, it's good of you to tell us all this."

A brief silence followed. Then he started explaining to us the rules of hygiene again. I realized that, in Le Chaâba, we practiced them very badly, but I did not say so.

"Now," he went on, after talking for half an hour, "you are all going to take off your socks and lay them flat on your desks, and I am going to check how clean each of you is."

A terrible anxiety gripped my throat. But it eased off quickly when I remembered that my mother had made me put on clean socks that morning. All around me there was total silence; then the pupils bent down to unlace their shoes. I did so too and stuck my nose in my socks to test the smell. Hm! OK. I won't look too ridiculous. Next to me, Jean-Marc laid on the table his perfectly colored nylon socks. Monsieur Grand went along each row, picking a sample here and there, taking care not to sniff them too closely, but turning them in all directions to look for stains and holes.

"Not very clean, this! . . . Very good here!" he said to

one or another of them. While some felt proud at being up to scratch, others were cursing themselves for not having thought to change their socks that morning.

Monsieur Grand reached Moussaoui and his crew. There were no socks on the desk.

"Moussaoui, take off your socks, and put them on the desk immediately," he said calmly.

Moussaoui hesitated for a few moments, looked at the window, and then finally decided to speak, staring at the teacher as he did so.

"I ain't taking my socks off. Why should I take them off, anyway? We ain't in the Health and Hygiene Department here. And, in any case, you're not my father. You can't boss me around. I ain't taking off my socks, so you're wasting your time here!"

Monsieur Grand's face suddenly turned red. He was completely stunned by the shock. It must have been the first time in his career as a teacher that he had had to deal with such a rebellion.

Moussaoui stood his ground, more determined than ever. Maybe he simply wanted to spare his opponent's nostrils?

"Your feet are dirty. That's why you don't want to take off your shoes," retorted the teacher, who, without realizing it, had started addressing Moussaoui in the disparaging *tu* form.

What happened afterward was beyond belief. Moussaoui, with a sickly smile on his face, cast him a withering look, then shouted:

"You old faggot! I don't give a shit about you."

An arctic chill descended on the class. We heard the

teacher mumble for a few seconds. He simply couldn't get his words out. He was completely at a loss. Moussaoui raised the stakes. He stood up, leaned his back against the window, standing sideways to the teacher, his fists tight, and shouted:

"If you want a fight, you faggot, come on, then. You don't scare me!"

Monsieur Grand could not even try to laugh off such a grotesque situation. He returned to his desk and, without looking at Moussaoui, said:

"We'll settle this in the headmaster's office."

My cousin sat down again with a relaxed look.

"The headmaster? Screw him," said Moussaoui. Then he added: "Why don't you all go screw yourselves, each and every one of you."

"You'll be expelled from school, you poor fool."

"You know where you can stick it, your school?"

"Right, that's enough now," said the teacher, "or I really am going to get angry."

"Go on, get angry," shouted the rebel, dancing about on both feet like Muhammad Ali. "Come on, then, come on, I'm ready for you!"

"We're going to have to lock this lunatic up!" Monsieur Grand suggested, turning toward the rest of the class.

"Faggot!" Moussaoui shouted again, hissing the *f* as emphatically as he could.

"Keep going! When your parents lose their family allowances, that'll teach you!"

These last words suddenly stunned Moussaoui. The argument packed a punch. He wasn't bothered about being expelled from school. But, if his father were to lose money because he refused to show his socks to the teacher, that was another matter! Fear spread across his face, and his eyes fell down to his desk in defeat. The stricken fighter mumbled a few more incomprehensible words; then suddenly a glimmer of light flashed through his body.

"You're all racists!" he screamed. "You can't stand us because we're Arabs!"

Monsieur Grand held the winning cards. He moved onto the attack:

"Don't try to defend yourself like that. The truth is you're a good-for-nothing and good-for-nothings like you never get anywhere in life."

"What a faggot!" said Moussaoui, turning toward Nasser. "He thinks we don't know why he always says we're last."

Nervous by nature, Nasser did not know where to look. The last thing he wanted to do was to have his parents lose their family allowances.

"Liar!" Monsieur Grand continued. "Look at Azouz." All eyes turned toward me. "He's an Arab too, and yet he is second in the class. So don't try making excuses. You are just a stupid good-for-nothing."

Monsieur Grand's remarks nailed me to my chair. Why me? Why had he decided to enlist me in his battle? Moussaoui sat there with his mouth open in front of his exercise book. He had been on the point of answering back, to prove to the teacher that he was a racist, when, wham! he was hit in the face by an incontrovertible truth. It was all over. He had nothing left. Checkmate! All because of me.

With the teacher's last words echoing round the classroom and in my head, the lesson was resumed. Monsieur Grand was speaking again as usual, but over there, in the donkeys' corner, as he called it, Moussaoui and his accomplices were talking loudly in Arabic, smiling and fidgeting in their seats. It was a textbook rebellion. But the teacher took no notice. I was completely out of it too. I wasn't listening to him. I was worrying about my cousins taking reprisals against me.

A few minutes later the bell shook me out of my torpor. As we moved toward the playground, some French children were talking in a low voice about the coup d'état staged by the Arabs at the back of the class. Once again I spurned the advances of Jean-Marc, who was pursuing his efforts to build an elitist pact with me.

"He's always causing problems for us, and then he says we're racists! I don't like that guy. What about you?" he asked.

"It's nothing to do with me!" I snapped.

Then he went off to join his compatriots.

I was heading toward Hacène, who was playing marbles in a corner of the playground, when Moussaoui came up to me, followed by his imperial guard. His eyes were blazing with hatred.

"What do you want now?" I said.

"Come over here. I need to talk to you."

We moved away from where the teachers and the head were standing together. I could see Monsieur

Grand among them telling them what had just happened to him.

"You see," said Moussaoui, "we're all Arabs, and we're not going to have *hachema* [shame] brought on us by some French faggot sniffing our socks in front of everyone."

"So what?"

"So what? . . . so what? You, you're the worst creep I've ever seen. When he asked you to take off your socks, what did you say? 'Yes, Sir, straight away.' Like some stupid girl."

"So?"

"Well, tell us why?"

"Well, it's because he's the teacher! And, anyway, I don't have a problem because my mother gave me brand-new socks this morning."

With Moussaoui showing signs of exasperation, Nasser came to his rescue:

"Look, we are all bottom of the class. OK?"

"Yeah."

"And why are we all bottom?"

"I dunno."

"Can't you see that the teacher's a racist? He doesn't like Arabs, I'm telling you."

"I dunno."

"Oh, yeah, how would he know?" put in Moussaoui. "After all, he's not an Arab."

The others agreed

"Of course I'm an Arab!"

"If you were, you'd be at the bottom of the class with us," said Moussaoui.

And Nasser went on:

"Yeah, yeah, why aren't ya at the bottom with us? He put you second, with the French kids, because you're not an Arab; you're a Gaouri like them."

"No, I am an Arab. I work hard; that's why I did well. Everyone can be like me."

A third ne'er-do-well intervened with the familiar question:

"Well, tell us why you're always with the French at break. Isn't it true you never hang around with us?"

The others were nodding in agreement. What could I say?

"See, you've nothing to say. 'Cos we're right. Yeah, you're French. OK, you look like an Arab like us, but you'd rather be French."

"No. It isn't true."

"That's enough; let's forget about him," said Moussaoui. "We don't talk to Gaouris."

Then they walked scornfully away from me as if they had just unmasked a spy.

I tried very hard to bounce back. I told myself that they were jealous of me. But I couldn't help feeling that Monsieur Grand had played a nasty trick on me. I was terribly ashamed by the accusations made against me by my fellow citizens because they were true. I was always playing with French kids during break. I wanted to be like them. I did everything Monsieur Grand told us to do.

Time moved slowly. In the afternoon the headmaster came to our classroom to fetch Moussaoui, and we never saw him again.

At the end of the afternoon, when I left school with the other gones from Le Chaâba, I said nothing. We returned to the shantytown in the usual way.

《 《 《

You're not an Arab! You're French! Fake! Creep! What on earth had I done to my fellow Arab kids? You're not an Arab! Of course I was! I was an Arab, and I could prove it: I had been circumcised just like them, three months earlier. It wasn't easy becoming an Arab, and there they were now, suspecting me of being an infidel.

Ah! My dear parents had thought they could hide from me the fact that my time had come, but I was no fool. Several days before the ceremony, they had started preparing us, Moustaf and me.

My mother repeated endlessly to her little lamb:

"Tell me, what are you going to do with all the money you're going to get? Will you let me have some? Aren't you lucky, my little lamb!"

You bet I was lucky! I would have gladly given up my turn for two cents worth of bread. I had already seen a gone mounting the scaffold and, while envying his sudden wealth, had concluded that it was definitely better to remain poor.

Four days before the fateful weekend the women had been busy preparing the couscous in enormous basins. My mother had used the one from which she had never been parted since El-Ouricia. While the couscous was being made, a festive atmosphere enveloped Le Chaâba. A dozen women settled down with their backs leaning against the wall of the shacks, sitting on their ample buttocks, with their left leg stretched out and the right one fully folded, thus enabling them to tightly grip the bowl in which the grains were rolled and gathered together. With sieves, water, salt, and semolina—everything was processed with rhythmic arm movements. One woman took care of the refreshments, moving around the workers offering coffee. The record player spewed out songs from the old country in Sétif, while the children hovered like flies around their mothers and the cakes that were served with the coffee.

The executioner was lined up.

By Friday evening the atmosphere was approaching its climax in Le Chaâba. Amid the rhythmic beat of the *bendirs* [drums], the women, separated from the men in a cousin's shack, were belly dancing, while the men gathered in our house, where they sat and talked about their lives in France. The children went backward and forward between the two parties, nibbling at what they found left and right.

I don't remember sleeping, I was so frightened. I kept asking my brother:

"Tell me, does it hurt?"

"I don't know anything about it; it's the first time for me too."

"How much dough do you think we'll get? What shall we do with it? I fancy buying a bike. Do you think dad will let me?"

Moustaf eventually fell asleep.

During the night I saw a hairy man coming toward me, brandishing a razor blade in his hand, sneering like a madman. When he put his murderous hand on my head, I jumped up in a supreme effort to free myself from his grasp. I awoke abruptly. My mother was there, standing in front of my bed with a smile. She had come to wake me up.

Saturday, seven o'clock in the morning. D-Day.

How could they call me a fake after all that I went through that day!

My mother bathed us in the family tub, put white shorts on each of us and a splendidly clean *gandoura* [robe] that reached down to our ankles. A green scarf was tied around our necks with several knots.

Nine o'clock in the morning. We were ready. We wandered around the shacks, haggard, anxious, awaiting the arrival of the *tahar* [circumciser]. Guests arrived, kissed us, and encouraged us with friendly pats on our heads. Wrapped in long multicolored binouars, wearing gold jewelry on their necks, wrists, bellies, and fingers, the women strode up and down in the courtyard.

On hearing that the tahar had arrived, my blood froze in my veins. A tall man, with the look of a European, with a moustache and brown suit "exclusively designed in the Villeurbanne flea market" and a tie that looked like it had been cut out of an old green curtain. He was carrying a briefcase. My father greeted him and led him into the main room, where a mattress had been placed on the floor, decorated with two enormous pillows covered in embroidered pillowcases.

The tahar summoned us. After a few soothing words, he lifted our gandouras up to our belly buttons, lowered our pants, and felt our bits of flesh.

"Everything is fine!" he concluded with a smile. "What's your name?"

"Azouz."

"You're a big boy, Azouz."

At lunchtime the guests tucked into the tons of couscous, vegetables, pieces of lamb, watermelon, dates, and pastries made from semolina and honey.

Two o'clock. The tahar had left the table to go into the execution room. Some men had followed him, taking us with them. The women were already there. Squatting in a corner, they were singing, beating the bendirs, and shouting themselves hoarse. Two chairs were placed near the window. The tahar prepared his instruments and other items. When he signaled to the men standing near me, my mother started crying.

Then four men seized me. In a fraction of a second I was lifted up onto the gallows, where my limbs were held down. Streams of tears sprang up from my eyes, and the lavender water that my mother sprinkled on my hair and my forehead served only to increase my anguish. Guests came up to me and furtively slipped banknotes into the knot of my green scarf, shouting their encouragement so they could be heard.

The tahar took my member between his fingers and pulled out the pink head. Seeing him do this, my anguish redoubled, and I cried out loudly. Then he pulled up all the extra skin to the front by pushing the head of my penis back with his thumb. I screamed, but the songs and the chants of the women drowned out the sound of my suffering.

"My son is a man; he doesn't cry," my father kept telling me.

Then the man in the suit, with one knee on the floor, took out his weapon: a pair of bright, thin, elongated chrome scissors. At the sight of this nightmarish vision my whole body seized up, my leg muscles swelled, and my eyes nearly came out of their sockets.

"Abboué, tell him to stop! Abboué, no, I don't want to! Stop! Stop! No . . ."

"That's very good, son; there's no need to cry," my father kept chanting.

I tried to move my body forward to escape the executioner's clutches. I folded my legs, then stretched them out violently in the hope of loosening the grip in which I was held. In vain.

Amid the throng of women pressed against each other, dripping with sweat, I recognized my mother. She was mopping her brow and her eyes with a handkerchief to wipe away the heat and the pain.

"Yemma! Yemma! Tell him I don't want him to cut me! Tell him I don't want it! Yemma, please!"

She turned her head away so she could cry more freely.

I spat on Bouchaoui, who was holding one of my legs. He smiled. I swore at everyone and cursed them. In vain.

The tahar gave me a nasty look, then shouted:

"Stop moving now, or I'll cut it all off."

I calmed down.

The two ends of the scissors tore into my flesh, and blood spurted out as if flowing from a broken dam. I was overwhelmed with pain while the tahar sprinkled some sort of coagulant powder on my gaping wound. Then he took me in his arms and placed me on the mattress. I don't remember anything else. My mother and several elderly women walked to the embankment singing ancient ritual songs and buried my bit of flesh along with some grains of couscous. It is still there.

I spent the next ten days without being able to put on any pants, without daring to pee for fear of losing what was left of my apparatus, ten days waddling like a duck to avoid anything rubbing. No, Cousin Moussaoui, I've earned my diploma as an Arab. I've paid my dues.

( ( (

In becoming a Muslim, I lost a bit of myself, but I gained a red bike. My father resisted for a long time because he had a great fear of such contraptions in view of our close proximity to the boulevard expressway. He would take the expressway on his moped on his way to work and knew it was dangerous.

"It's mine; the money is mine," I said to him, pointing to the money I had received on the day of my circumcision. "You told me I could buy what I want with it. Well, I'm going to get a bike!"

"You pay me back all the money I spent on hospitality for everyone, and I'll let you have the money the guests gave you."

Thus, it seemed, my father dashed my hopes of ever riding a bike.

But some time later he returned from work with a red bike strapped on the rear mudguard of his moped.

I spent a quarter of an hour kissing him, promised him that I would never go further than the embankment, that I would never ride it on the expressway, and that I would work even harder at school to please him.

On hearing this last argument, he responded:

"Oh, no, my son. If you work at school, that's for you, not for me. It's your life you're preparing for, not mine."

I took the red bike and did a trial run under his anxious gaze.

"Look! You can see I know how to do it."

"Yes, yes, I see. But put it away now; you're going to ruin it."

"No, not yet, Abboué, not yet. Look, here I am; I'm not going far."

"Put it away," he said. "Don't start."

I obeyed, but slowly, to show my annoyance. Father was already beginning to get on my nerves.

During the following weeks I was not allowed to use my bike as I wanted to. My mother was put under pressure not to let me take it out when the head of the household was absent. That was why, at the first opportunity, when Rabah suggested going to get some fodder for his rabbits in Vaulx-en-Velin, I waited until she went to l'bomba before sneaking out on my bike.

There were six of us riding along the boulevard, a major highway, trying to race each other. We lost track of the distance and time, so intoxicated were we by the speed, the asphalt, the big cars overtaking us, and the places we passed. Nothing else mattered, not even Bouzid. On the way back we went by Villeurbanne to see the *vogue* [fair] and then the hookers. We had a pretty full day.

It was dark when we got back to Le Chaâba. In the dusk Bouzid was waiting for us, his hands crossed behind his back. We could not see his face. A few feet away more men and women were waiting. I recognized my mother among them. She seemed terrified.

My legs started turning to jelly. When my father came toward me, I put two hands on my head to protect me from the oncoming blow, but nothing happened. He simply barked out the command:

"Gimme your *filou* [bike]!"

Without trying to understand, and only too happy to get out of it so easily, I got off my bike and handed it to him nervously. I was still on my guard.

He went over to the others:

"Get off, you too. And you. And you."

He said the same to Rabah:

"And you, as well. Come on, get off, or I'll knock you off."

The gone must have been busy grinning his usual grin, the one he used to demonstrate his arrogance, and he was not quick enough to avoid the terrible punch my father directed at his cheek. His grin disappeared. His mother and father were speechless.

Bouzid then grabbed all the bikes, piled them up in the middle of Le Chaâba under our incredulous eyes, took up a sledgehammer that he had brought along for the purpose, quietly and steadily lifted it above his head, then brought it crashing down several times, until there was nothing left of our brightly colored filous except our memories of them.

As my bike was at the bottom of the pile, I hoped there might be something left of it. When I saw the full extent of the wreck, I clenched my teeth so I would not show my bitterness. I had given up my bit of flesh for nothing.

( ( (

Now that there were no more bikes in Le Chaâba I stayed home on the days when we had no school. My father wouldn't let us go to the market any more or to the banks of the Rhône or to the boulevard. Our last escapade had been too much for him. My mother complained more and more, and her moufissa seemed to be getting worse all the time.

One morning she decided to wash herself in the green tub. The water had been boiling on the stove for a while.

Yemma took off her binouar and settled her heavy frame in the tub. She was like a newborn baby, nice and plump, kneeling in a tiny bowl. Zohra started pouring warm water from a can on her hair so that she could work the shampoo in. The liquid spilled onto the lino.

"Gently! You're going to drown me!"

Zohra turned toward me, with an ironic grin on her face.

Mother was angry:

"You think this is funny, do you?"

Then she said to me:

"And you? What are you looking at? Come on, get out!"

It was to be expected. I always seemed to be in the wrong. When I stayed at home, I was told to go out, and, when I was out, I was told to come in.

Hacène was walking past the window. He signaled to me to join him.

"What're you doing?"

"Nothing, I was just going out."

"How about going fishing in the Rhône?"

"Are you mad or what? My father will kill me."

"You scared?"

"Course I'm scared! Look at the marks on my ass. I got 'em the last time we went to the Rhône, when my father came to find us."

Now he understood my hesitation. He made another suggestion:

"Well, we could go to the cabin; we won't stay long if you like."

We set off toward Louise's house. A couple of kids were throwing stones at the sign that read: "Embankment. No dumping of garbage. Offenders will be fined." A missile hit the target, making a noise like a gong.

A little further on Saïda was taking her little brother for a ride in his stroller. She was wearing the high-heeled shoes she had found the week before in some garbage discharged by a truck. She was walking like a grown-up lady. Hacène spoke to her while lifting up her skirt.

"You idiot! Stop it, or I'll tell your mother!"

"Oh, ain't she stupid! We can't even have a bit of fun."

Then, turning toward me, he said:

"Come on, let's go to the cabin."

Saïda joined in the conversation.

"Are you going to the cabin? Can I come too?"

"If you want," replied Hacène. "You can do the housework while we go fishing."

"OK! Wait for me."

She ran quickly home to deposit her brother and returned straight away, excited at the thought of joining the boys. On the way there, Hacène kept fondling her ass, and she protested less and less.

The cabin was still there, nestling in the hollow of the oak tree. Saïda put together a makeshift broom with some branches and started cleaning the inside. A few minutes later she stopped, then came to sit cross-legged right opposite me.

I asked her:

"What shall we do?"

"Shall we tell Toto stories?" suggested Hacène. "I know one! Toto and Search-me are in a boat. Toto falls in the water. Who's left?"

"Search-me!" called out Saïda, very pleased with herself at finding the answer.

I pinched her ass.

"You stupid jerk!"

We burst out laughing. She got cross.

"I'm going."

I held her back by her dress.

"No, wait. Look. Have you ever seen a tool that's been cut? Do you want to see mine?"

"No. That's disgusting!"

"No. You can't see anything now. It's healed."

After undoing my fly, I took out my tackle and showed her every bit of it. She seemed interested.

"You can see it's not dirty."

"Yeah, I saw."

"Why don't we get it on like grown-ups?"

She blushed nervously, while Hacène encouraged her, in spite of his surprise:

"Oh, ya. Let's get it on like grown-ups."

"OK. But what if my mother sees us?"

I reassured her.

"Your mother isn't here. And, besides, we won't tell anyone anything. Take off your undies!"

After a hesitating for a moment, she took them off.

"And what do we do now?"

I went up to her, holding my *zénana*. Then Saïda sat down, opened her legs, and offered me a private show. I delicately laid my hammer on her anvil and waited, in that strange position, for something to happen. What exactly? I hadn't the slightest idea.

"So what do we do now?" asked Saïda.

"Nothing," I said. "We get it on, and that's it!"

Hacène interjected after following the lesson studiously.

"Me too, I want to get it on."

He unsheathed his equipment and imitated me.

"Is this what our parents do?" asked the girl.

Neither of us answered.

After a few moments, satisfied that he too had got it on, Hacène pulled up his pants, looking very serious.

Suddenly a voice rang out clearly through the tree trunks in the forest. It came from Le Chaâba.

"Saïda! Saïda!"

The girl immediately cried:

"It's my mother."

She pulled her undies back on, straightened her dress, and begged us one last time:

"You won't tell, will you?"

"No, no, don't worry," I said along with Hacène.

She disappeared behind the trees.

The very next day all the gones in Le Chaâba knew that Saïda had let us get it on with her.

((( (

As we were walking to school one day we came across two Peugeot 404 police cars and a paddy wagon heading for Le Chaâba.

"They're going to our place," shouted Rabah.

We all ran home behind the vehicles, which were going slowly because of the potholes in the road.

They stopped at the entrance to Le Chaâba, and some uniformed men rushed to the gate. One of them, no doubt a police inspector, asked:

"Who's in charge here?"

Hacène came closer to me.

"I bet they've come about the hookers."

"I doubt it."

"Maybe we've been informed on by one of the customers whose windshield we broke."

"You could be right after all."

"Now, then, is there no one there who can speak French?" the inspector shouted through the gate.

Then he signaled to three policemen, who immediately took a close look all the way round Le Chaâba.

The inspector stared at us in a far from friendly way.

Two women, one of whom was my mother, came to the gate. Their heads were wrapped in bath towels for reasons of decorum.

The inspector explained the purpose of his visit:

"You've got illegal slaughterhouses here. Where are they?"

The women remained silent. They raised their open hands toward the sky to show they knew nothing.

"Sheep . . . butcher's . . . kwkkkk . . . kwkkkk," said the police inspector, miming the movement of a knife slitting an animal's throat.

This time my mother understood.

"Dunno. Me no speak French. No undestan'."

The inspector was losing his patience, irritated by the way my mother kept saying: "No undestan'! No undestan'!"

"You're all the same. You never understand French when the police are around."

Then, turning toward a colleague, he added:

"It's only when they want something that they can speak French. Come on, let's make a start. You two, over that way. You, over here. The others with me."

The policemen went in and searched everywhere from top to bottom. Nothing. There was not the slightest smell of sheep to be detected. Not the smallest ball of wool to feel. They came out and looked at us from head to toe. When he got back to the gate, the inspector took another look at his suspects. I shuddered. The inspector smiled, took three steps toward me, looked straight into my eyes, and said:

"Do you go to school, young man?"

"Yes, M'sieur."

"Which school do you go to?"

"The Ecole Léo-Lagrange, M'sieur."

"Do you work hard at Ecole Léo-Lagrange?"

"Yes, M'sieur. Now I am among the best in the class. Before . . ."

The inspector interrupted me:

"That's good. It's important to work hard at school, you know. One day, you too can become a police inspector if you want. But, you know, you'll have to make people respect the law. Do you think you'll be able to do that?"

"Of course, Sir. At school, we learn all about behaving properly."

"Do you? Then you could become a great inspector. Now, can you tell me where the sheep are slaughtered here?"

"Yes, Sir. I know where. My uncle is the butcher. He kills the sheep behind the shacks at the bottom of the garden. Can you see the apple tree over there? Well, it's just behind it."

"You lead the way and show me how to get there, my young future inspector."

Proud of myself, and under the astonished gaze of the women of Le Chaâba, I led the representatives of law and order to the pool of dried blood. Above it hung the hooks from which my uncle would hang the carcasses when cutting them into pieces. Some freshly shorn sheepskins were strewn here and there, waiting to be processed. They gave off a horrible smell, which the inspector couldn't stand.

Two policemen approached. One of them took a camera out of its case and photographed the installation from all angles. I couldn't understand what they were doing.

"Come on, let's go," ordered the inspector.

As he went past the women who had been watching the scene, he handed my mother a piece of paper on which he had hastily scribbled a few words.

"Give this to the owner of the house. It is a summons for him to report to the Villeurbanne police station. This evening before six o'clock. Understood?"

My mother still didn't understand French. She raised her arms, as if to surrender. The inspector then turned toward me.

"You can read, can't you?"

"Yes, Sir."

"Then read out what's on this paper to the owner of the house."

"My father is the owner, Sir."

"Well, tell him to come this evening before six o'clock, with your uncle the butcher, to the Villeurbanne police station. You'll be a big boy, won't you?"

He winked at me.

"Yes, Inspector. I'll tell that all to my father."

The uniformed men went back into their vehicles and drove off toward the boulevard. They had hardly disappeared down the track when Zidouma jumped on me, her fangs out:

"You idiot, couldn't you keep your mouth shut? You did it on purpose, didn't you? You did, didn't you?"

She pulled my hair and shook my head. It seemed I must have done something really serious. My mother intervened:

"Leave my son alone. I forbid you to lay your hands on him. It's not his fault. You can see he's too young to understand. Anyway, it serves you right. You're carrying on an illegal activity here; tomorrow all the papers will be talking about us, and now you want to hit my son! You'd better not, I'm telling you."

"You're jealous," said Zidouma, "because my husband earns more money than yours thanks to the slaughterhouse."

"I don't want to talk to you any more. The men will sort this problem out between them this evening," my mother retorted, pushing me from behind to make me go inside the house.

The inspector had really landed me in it.

( ( (

I was lying on the floor, absorbed in reading my book, when my father returned home. Visibly uneasy, my mother did not look at him but extracted from his bag the tin box in which he usually carried his lunch; then she went to rinse it in the basin.

He sat down after hanging his jacket on the door handle, then got up and stuck his hand into one of the pockets. He came toward me and handed me a packet of candies, without a trace of emotion on his lips.

"Here, this is for you."

I took his present, and he went and sat down again.

I got up to give him a kiss on the cheek, and then he smiled.

"Now don't be greedy. Share them with your brothers and sisters."

My mother came back, still not daring to look at him.

"Bring me my coffee."

"Yes. I'm just doing it."

Zohra called:

"It's OK, Mom, I'm already doing it."

My mother started to walk toward the kitchen, hesitated, and then turned around to announce gravely:

"The *boulicia* [police] were here this afternoon."

"What are you talking about? The boulicia? Why would the boulicia come here? To my house?"

My mother said nothing when faced with this avalanche of questions. I stopped reading, while Zohra continued to stir the coffee in the pot, all the while looking at my father.

"Come on, woman, speak! What disaster has befallen us, in Allah's name?"

"It's all because of Saïd's sheep. They came about his sheep. They wanted to know where the sheep were slaughtered. Azouz showed them the spot."

A strange glimmer flashed from his eyes. He shouted:

"You can't flirt with the devil and get away with it. That man is a demon. I should never have let him kill animals on my land. I'm getting what I deserve. I'm the one to blame. Now he can go stuff his sheep."

Swearing loudly, he got up as if to go out. Then my mother landed the knockout blow:

"You have to go to the *koussaria* [police station] this evening with him."

"What? I have to go to the koussaria? I've never had any dealings with the boulicia. They'll force us out of here now, like dogs. What a brother! What a bearer of misfortune! Why did I not leave you behind in El-Ouricia?"

My mother had taken refuge in the kitchen, trembling with fear.

"You, stop stirring that spoon, Zohra. Can't you see the coffee's spilling over? We've got enough problems as it is."

Consumed with violent hatred, Bouzid left the house, determined to make his brother pay for the misfortune that had befallen us. I followed him.

"Where is he, the demon? Where is the dog hiding?" he shouted at Zidouma as he pushed the shack door open with his foot.

"In the garden!" she replied, her head held up in defiance.

"You're all the same," he shouted in her face before slamming the door behind him.

Saïd was there, in his butcher's yard, hastily cutting up the remaining pieces of the sheep discovered by the police, no doubt anxious to sell them before reporting to the police station.

"You swine! Because of you I've had the boulicia knocking at my door. Have you no honor, no shame, to do such a thing to me! Damn you. Allah will make you pay for your sins."

He grabbed every piece of meat, threw them all into the mud, and trampled them under his feet as if they were his brother.

"Don't ever expect anything from me. You disgust me. Get out! Get out! Take your family, your furniture, your shack. Get out of my sight!" he screamed, as he began to demolish the workshop.

Saïd covered his eyes and swallowed hard. By what power did he manage to stop himself from laying his hands on his older brother? It was impossible! Unimaginable! You couldn't raise your hand against the head of Le Chaâba, even if he hit you where it hurt most.

Bouzid left the garden, stumbling over a sheepskin that was still drying on the ground. He gave it a violent kick. The skin wrapped itself around his shoe.

"Go home, you! What are you doing here?" he shouted at me.

Zidouma was waiting at l'bomba. When she saw my father coming, she stared at him for the first time in her life, her mouth drooping, her nose screwed up, and her eyes filled with hate.

She dared to take him on.

"Who do you think you are? Allah in person? We're not your slaves. You're human like the rest of us. And not even that. A human being would never have done what you did to my husband. Too much is too much. You've always been against us. I guess you're jealous of him. It was your son who told the boulicia everything. He's the one you should be beating up."

"Go back home, woman! This is none of your business!"

"No, I won't go back home. I'm free to do as I like."

"I'm telling you to get back into your hole. Otherwise I'll make you!"

"I said no! Hit me then! Go on, hit me!"

On hearing these words my father unleashed himself on her without any restraint, grabbing her by the hair to drag her back into her shack. The neighbors came out, panic-stricken by all the shouting and children crying. Three men surrounded my father.

"She wants to be a man now, this cow. Listen to her; she's insulting me. Let go of me. I am going to cut her throat; I'm going to drink her blood."

Zidouma, as if possessed by the devil, was swearing even louder, cursing, and threatening to burn us all alive at the stake.

After a few minutes they finally managed to separate the belligerents and shut them in their respective cages. Some men stayed with my father. My mother and my sisters were crying. I was crying too, bewildered.

( ( (

"Read it all to me quickly."

"But if I read in French, you won't understand anything," replied Zohra, suggesting to my father that she should translate into Arabic the main ideas from the article that the local paper had written about us.

"I understand French better than you. Do you take me for an ass or something? Read everything, I am telling you, word for word. Whatever you do, don't leave anything out!"

Zohra obeyed. She knew full well that he would not understand anything.

"'During a search conducted on Tuesday afternoon in a shantytown in Villeurbanne, police from Villeurbanne discovered a large meat-trafficking operation conducted by North Africans. There, in deplorably unhygienic conditions, sheep were slaughtered before being cut up and sold, without any statutory control, to a North African clientele living mainly in the prefabs along the Boulevard Laurent-Bonnevay.

"'The shrewdness of the police combined with painstaking work has enabled them to put an end to the activities of these outlaws. Heavy fines were imposed on M. Bouzid . . . and M. Saïd. . . .'"

"Are they talking about me?"

"I think so."

"Carry on!"

"That's all."

"Are you sure?"

"Yes, look. I've got up to here, the end of this line."

With her trembling finger, Zohra pointed to the end of the article. While she had been reading, my father had stood in front of her, his eyes half closed in order to take in the words more fully, his ear fixed on the reader.

"And this, what's this?" he went on, pointing to another article.

"That's something else, that. It isn't about us. It finishes here."

"I don't believe you! Carry on reading!"

"There's no point. It's about sport!"

"*Di zbour?* Are you trying to make fun of me? Read, I said."

"'Olympique Lyonnais 3–Marseilles 1. A deserved victory,'" Zohra continued, crying.

"Are you crying? You're hiding something from me."

Moustaf, who had been listening since the beginning, intervened:

"Abboué. She's right; that's all there is. They're talking about soccer now."

"*L'ballou?* [Soccer?] ok, that's enough for now," said father.

Zohra withdrew into the kitchen, exhausted by her ordeal.

"You can't ask women to do anything; they cry for no reason. But you're all scheming against me, aren't you?" insisted Bouzid.

Then, turning toward Moustaf, he said:

"Translate for me what they're saying in the paper!"

Moustaf did a rough translation of the important words in the article.

"*L'bidoufile* [shantytown] . . . What does that mean, *le bidoufile?*"

"It's what they call Le Chaâba, Abboué!"

"Why do they call us *le bidoufile?*"

"I really don't know."

My brother was clearly bewildered by my father's questions. He folded the paper in half and placed it on the table, then left the room. Bouzid picked it up, leafed through it, recognized the article, and stared at it, grimacing.

"Bidoufile . . . trafficking . . . sheep. They are talking about me, Bouzid, in the paper. All the French people are going to know about me now. How shameful! The boulicia are going to put us under surveillance. I know how they do things. They'll hassle us until we're thrown out. 'Go back where you came from.' That's what they'll say. I know the French. And all this is Saïd's fault! But Allah will punish him, and only him."

Turning his head toward the wall separating us from our cousins' shack, he went on:

"And on top of that his old hag wanted to raise her hand against me! Damn them both!"

There was a knock on the door.

"Come in, Bouchaoui, come in! Come and have a coffee with me. Have you read the paper? We're done for, don't you think?"

Bouchaoui, looking serious, sat down next to him and took a coffee.

"Are they talking about us in the newspaper?"

"Yes, look. It's talking about Le Chaâba, about me. My name is there! They wrote my name in the newspaper. It's the worst scandal of my life."

"It's shameful for all of us, Bouzid, not just you. Listen, as I was returning home from work, on the way the police stopped me to check my papers. I handed them my card. They laughed at me and called me a dune coon. It's going to be like that every day now. I don't like it. My kids have stopped working at school. My wife is always complaining. And there's nothing I can do except work, work, work. What a mess, Bouzid!"

My mother, who had not dared approach her husband since he returned home, finally came to greet Bouchaoui.

"Come on, come and eat, both of you."

"No, thanks, I am going to get back home."

"Come on, come on. You are here now, you must stay," insisted Bouzid. "You'll share our dinner, even if there isn't much of it."

The two men talked gloomily long after dinner, until all the lights in Le Chaâba had gone out.

( ( (

Months went by. Before then Le Chaâba had survived the wars of l'bomba, the battles between rival clans, and the hookers, but the scandal of the illegal slaughterhouse proved to be fatal. Zidouma had gone too far. She broke one of the final taboos.

Surrounded by the friends in her clan, she became known as the one who had dared. The Daring One, full stop. Since then she had felt strong, encouraged by those who had been waiting for the opportunity to challenge the authority of the master of Le Chaâba. Zidouma had won. Half the shantytown now belonged to her, listened to her, and supported her decisions.

My mother suffered terribly.

Saïd had stopped slaughtering his sheep in Le Chaâba, but he somehow continued to deliver his cutlets, legs of lamb, and steaks on his moped. He almost never saw Bouzid now, taking care to arrive home after him. But he no longer bore a grudge. No. Hatred had faded away, giving way to indifference, a terrible indifference that was eating into the soul of Le Chaâba.

⟨ ⟨ ⟨

Early one morning, as I struggled to open my eyes under the harsh light of the rising sun, I was suddenly intrigued by a peculiar commotion. The Bouchaoui family was gathered all together, some distance away, at the pump. Some suitcases and several boxes clumsily tied with string stood in the middle of the yard. The children were wearing their Sunday best. Maybe because Sunday was the Lord's day, but that wasn't the usual practice in our neck of the woods.

Monsieur Bouchaoui was moving busily between his shack, not far from the privy, and the spot where he had placed the luggage. Around him several men and women were talking. I went up to them to find out what had happened that night. Why was Bouchaoui emptying his shack like that? Maybe he was just giving his dwelling a good spring cleaning? Who knows, perhaps he had decided to put in fitted carpets?

"There! I've finished. When it comes down it, I'm not taking much, and I won't have to make a second trip with the taxi," Bouchaoui said to Bouzid.

The Bouchaouis were leaving. They were leaving Le Chaâba to go and live in Lyon, in a real building. Two men carried the suitcases and boxes up to the main gate.

"If you have forgotten something, it won't be lost," my father said, struggling to hide his bitterness.

"God knows if I will ever come back. I prefer to let you have everything I am leaving here."

The generous Monsieur Bouchaoui was bequeathing all his expensive furniture to us: an old wardrobe with crooked corners infested with woodworm, a table with more dirt and layers of paint than wood, and two wobbly chairs from which the stuffing had long since disappeared and been replaced by plywood.

"You do what you like with them. Sell them if you can," suggested Bouchaoui, as if he were he giving up a part of himself.

"You know I don't need your stuff. It'll die where you've left it."

"No, no, Bouzid. I owe you something. You welcomed me here with my family for years. You found me work with your boss, and I never gave you a dinar to thank you."

"What are you talking about, Bouchaoui? What do you want me to do with your money?"

"Nothing. That's why I am leaving you my furniture!"

"You are as stubborn as a herd of mules. Well, leave your bits of furniture there if you insist!"

"The taxi's here! The taxi's here!" called out the gones, who had been impatiently awaiting the arrival of the car since they were told that it was coming to collect the Bouchaoui family.

It was the first time that one of us folks had traveled in such style.

The driver came up to the spot where he could see the luggage.

"Did someone here call a taxi?"

"*Oui, Missiou!* [Yes, Monsieur!]," my father confirmed.

"Is that the luggage there? Is that all you've got?"

"*Oui, Missiou! Trois falises y dou cartoux. Si tau!* [Yes, Monsieur! Three suitcases and two boxes. That's all!]"

The driver didn't look too happy, but he loaded the Bouchaouis' riches into the trunk.

While this was happening I looked into the vehicle: what luxury! Fitted carpet underfoot and on the sides, velvet seats, all around the smell of a new car, such a clean smell! And to think that the Bouchaouis were going to ride in it!

Then came the kisses and the tears. Everybody promised to keep in touch.

Madame Bouchaoui disappeared in the back with her three children, her legs entangled in her binouar, which she refused to swap for a French skirt. Monsieur Bouchaoui sat next to the driver, visibly moved by the softness of the seat on which he had just sat.

"Where are you going?" asked the driver.

"*A l'angar Birache,*" Bouchaoui ordered.

"Where?"

"*A l'angar Birache.*"

"Do you mean to the Perrache station?" the driver grimaced.

"Yes. *A l'angar Birache,*" Bouchaoui confirmed as he waved to us through the car window.

The taxi moved off, taking the Bouchaoui family far away from Le Chaâba.

"May Allah be with you!" said my father.

He returned to the empty shack. My mother followed him. She asked him:

"Do you want to give it to somebody else?"

"No. There are already too many of us. This shack will now remain empty. I'll knock it down soon."

The Bouchaouis' departure puzzled me and left a bitter taste in my mouth. I asked my father:

"Abboué, why did the Bouchaouis leave?"

"Well, it was Allah's will. That's all."

"Weren't they happy here?"

"I imagine not, since they've left."

"Had you known for a while that they were leaving?"

"No. I learned about it this morning. Oh, stop harassing me with your stupid questions. Go and find something else to do."

〈 〈 〈

For all of us left in Le Chaâba, daily life became heavy and dull. The atmosphere became leaden as if the sky had wrapped itself in a blanket of gray-black clouds.

Leaving. A lot of people started thinking about leaving. Where to? Anywhere.

The Bouchaouis' shack was still standing. Stubbornly it still clung to the others, soulless. The crimson wallpaper, hung up hastily on the planks to create an illusion of something beautiful, became worn with the passage of time, letting in drafts from which no one had anything to fear except for me and some other gones who went there from time to time on a Thursday.

The previous afternoon a garbage truck had come to unload its riches in the usual way on the embankment by the banks of the Rhône. No one bothered to announce its arrival. No one clung on to its sides. No one ran behind it to secure a place on the garbage heap. There were now only half a dozen young scavengers lost amid the vast field of treasure. There was no longer any need to hold onto your place; there were no more fights, no more jealous scenes. Scavenging for the sake of scavenging had become pointless. Suddenly I stopped rummaging among the garbage, abandoning no doubt fabulous treasures to the depths of the dump. I returned home.

My mother was stitching a pillowcase, and Zohra was doing the ironing. One of them was in the kitchen while the other was in the main room. They were chatting.

"They said they were leaving a long time ago," said Zohra.

"She must be happy now," said my mother, no doubt talking about Zidouma.

"Who ya talking about?" I asked curiously.

"None of your business. This is women's talk!"

"I wanna know. Tell me; otherwise I'll tell Dad everything."

"What do you think you're going to tell Dad? Have you gone crazy or something?"

"I'm gonna tell him everything! I'm not telling you what!"

"You're an idiot. If you really want to know, we were talking about the Bouchaouis."

"Well, why didn't you tell me earlier?"

"OK, now stop it. Leave us alone to talk in peace. Go and play outside!"

Then Zohra spoke to my mother again:

"Yemma, do you think Madame Bouchaoui has got a house with everything now? Tap water? Electricity? Toilet?"

"How should I know? I don't know anything about it."

"What was it like at El-Ouricia?"

"Over there we had even less than here. Do you think your father came here for fun?"

I listened closely as my mother recounted her life while Zohra, hungry for details, constantly interrupted.

"Yemma, do you think we're going to leave here too?"

"You're asking too many questions, my daughter, and you haven't finished your ironing. God alone knows where we will be tomorrow."

Zohra could see that her mother didn't want to talk any more and that she wanted to be alone.

"Go on, put the washing away quickly. HE is here."

That was how she referred to my father when talking to her daughters: as "HE."

For several weeks now, HE had been shutting himself away at home as soon as he returned to Le Chaâba. "*Salam oua rlikoum* [Good-day to you]" here, "*Salam oua rlikoum*" there, then each to his own shack.

My mother was more and more fearful when she saw him. When he sat like a statue in his chair, ordered his black potion, and kneaded his chewing tobacco between his fingers with the meticulousness of an old man, she had to stop herself from telling him to go out, to go and breathe some fresh air and chat with the other men.

If she had made such a suggestion, Bouzid would not have beaten her. No, he would have simply told her that Le Chaâba was no longer what it was, that the men no longer gathered together in the yard to drink coffee and listen to the radio as they used to before, that now he was avoiding the others for he had nothing more to share with them. Le Chaâba had changed. No. HE would not have beaten my mother. Maybe he simply wouldn't have answered; that would have been all.

But I was dreaming. Messaouda was incapable of speaking like that to her husband. And HE never expressed his feelings.

( ( (

Le Chaâba's soul was slipping away through the cracks in the planks. The shack occupied by our cousins, who had just gone, was still leaning against our house, now lonely and empty.

When Saïd, Zidouma, Rabah, and Hacène left, I did not eat for two days. I did not cry. I did what my mother, Moustaf, and Zohra did. They were no doubt as upset as I was at the sight of our cousins leaving, but none of them let the slightest emotion show through. In any case, since that business with the meat Rabah had been avoiding us, spending his Thursdays with gones from the prefabs. Something profound had already disappeared from our lives. I did not cry.

Now we were alone, abandoned in the ruins of Le Chaâba.

Old Ma Louise walked in, forgetting even to knock on the door. With a smile, she asked my mother:

"So, my beautiful? How are you? *Labaisse ou labaisse pas?* [You OK or not?]"

"*Labaisse, labaisse* [I'm fine, I'm fine]," my mother answered while continuing to roll her couscous grains, sitting cross-legged in the kitchen.

Zohra said loudly in Arabic:

"She has come to eat couscous again."

Ma Louise never liked us speaking Arabic in front of her. A few years back she would have slapped Zohra in the face and deprived her of her afternoon treat for a week. But today she said nothing. She looked fragile. She put her hand in her pocket and took out her cigarette case. She tapped her filterless Gauloise four times on the back of her hand in order to pack down the tobacco and looked straight into Zohra's eyes as she asked her for a light. This Gaouria was now the only neighbor my mother had during the day, when we were at school, and she had become too much. Intrusive.

My mother had never spoken French. Well, a little. With the milkman, who used to come twice a week to bring milk and butter to Le Chaâba. At the sound of his horn she used to come out with the other women and repeat in French the words her children had taught her. She made everybody laugh, including the milkman, for whom I had to translate the order.

"Give me *li zou*," she would say.

"Yemma, *les zeux* [the eggs]," I corrected her each time

"*Li zou.* Oh, leave me alone to say it how I want. He understands me, don't worry," she said.

The milkman would always smile. After a while he had ended up learning Chaâba-style Arabic.

Nowadays, the milkman no longer came to Le Chaâba. He had no more customers. My mother had forgotten her French, and in any case she didn't like talking in French, with Dame Louise or anyone else. She felt trapped by her neighbor. Could she just stand there and say nothing? Louise was alone, pitiful behind the cloud of smoke emanating from her mouth. She would come to our house to feel less lonely, to be with her friends in Le Chaâba, to hear them, speak with them, order them about, "show them her clout," and select guests for afternoon tea.

My mother's spirits were already too low for her to be able to offer solace to her neighbor. She was also afraid of being pitied, that the Gaouria might think: "The old beauty is lonely; she needs me." She did not want to be pitied. Did she need to be pitied? True, she would be lying if she said she was happier than before, but she was OK, she was not unhappy. "*Labaisse tou labaisse!* [Fine, everything was fine!]"

"Have you heard from the Bouchaouis?" asked the former commander in chief of Le Chaâba.

"*Ria di to!*"

"*Rien du tout?* [Nothing at all?]"

"*Ria di to!* No!"

"What about the others?"

"No one has come back to see us," Zohra interjected,

realizing that her mother didn't want to answer any more of Louise's questions.

Then mother spoke to her daughter in Arabic, asking her to repeat her words to the Frenchwoman.

"Tell her: In what other Chaâba will the men be able to pray in the fields or in the garden without looking ridiculous? To what other place can they go to celebrate the *Aïd*? And what are they going to do for circumcisions? And where are they going to slaughter their sheep? They will come back. And the women? Where are they going to hang out their washing?"

Zohra translated her mother's arguments word for word.

Le Chaâba was ours, and my mother needed to say it to herself again and again so as not to suffer. But she was suffering all the same.

"Yes, you are home here. You'll never find another place like this," repeated Louise, stubbing the tip of her Gauloise under her shoe.

She went on:

"Well, I gotta go. I gotta make the soup for Gu and Pollo."

Ma Louise had hardly left when my father returned home. He was expressionless and badly shaven, yet his still bright eyes showed no sign of weakness since the demise of Le Chaâba. Le Chaâba didn't exist any more; there was now just a house. His house. Bouzid hadn't really understood what had happened. He didn't stop to think why everyone else had fled from his paradise. He carried on with his chewing tobacco and with everything else in his life just as before.

Meanwhile I fell asleep every night begging Allah the Great to send down an angel to tell my father that we were all unhappy, that we wanted to follow those who had left, that we were miserable because of them.

Time dragged on, monotonous and uneventful. No celestial envoy came knocking on our door. Autumn only compounded the sadness enveloping Le Chaâba, which by now had been empty for months.

Baudelaire! Yes! That wretched autumn made me think of Baudelaire. Monsieur Grand had made us learn one of Baudelaire's poems by heart, a poem in which he painted the melancholia of that season. At the time I thought that the poet must have been going through a lot of hassle to write such sad words. But now I saw things differently when I looked at the apple and the plum trees, all bare in the garden, hideous, with branches like barbed wire poking out like snakes from the heap of rotten planks, mangled corrugated iron, and rusty oil drums strewn across the ground at their feet. Even the Bouchaouis' furniture ended up laid to rest there.

A pile of building materials for a shantytown! That was all there was left of Le Chaâba.

But how could we tell him? How could we open his eyes? He would have to read Baudelaire. But who was going to teach him to read? There was nothing to be done. In any case poetry would not open his heart. Did he even have a heart like ours? Maybe Zidouma was right. But what about the packets of candies he had brought me lately? No, you couldn't say he didn't have a heart. He did have a heart, but unfortunately it was unpredictable. Sometimes it took a break. It was capricious. He could seem cold, without pity, without affection. Bouzid was like a man with a roaming heart. At present it was made of stone. You couldn't get through to him. He wouldn't let anyone talk about moving house. He said nothing and showed no trace of emotion. His heart had gone off on annual leave. If only it had gone off some other time!

Oh, Yemma, if you hadn't been there, who could I have complained to? To whom could I sing the lament of the haunted house? Father didn't like modern music. Now you, Mother, were my final hope for getting out of this nightmare.

Poor mother! One day I harassed her with my usual chorus, and she ended up sobbing for minutes on end, cursing herself, moaning about her wretched life.

"Oh, God, what have I done to you to deserve so much suffering? He makes me cry every evening, and my children take it out on me, they torture me. Oh, God, please let me die," she whispered.

I felt like my soul had become that of a murderer, like the executioner who had stolen my bit of flesh. I abandoned the idea of moving house and gave my mother a big hug.

"I'm sorry, Yemma. I don't want to move any more. I swear I'll never cry again. Stop crying, Yemma. Please."

Her torrent of sorrow flowed all the faster.

( ( (

"I'm sick of being in these shacks! I want to move! I'm sick of being in these shacks! I want to move!"

Every evening, when he came home, I sang him this

enchanting chorus—while he was eating, while he was drinking his coffee, while he was listening to the radio. He ignored me. He did not even bother to look at me. So I sang my song faster. I moaned. He remained impassive. As a precaution I always stood a few yards away from him so that he could not lay his fat, heavy hand on me. Just in case . . .

The wind could blow to its heart's content and unleash the most dreadful of gales, but it made no difference. Bouzid and his house were imprisoned in each other.

He settled down in his usual seat, endlessly repeating the same movements with his coffee and his tobacco box. One evening he even fell asleep at the table with his jacket still on.

I settled down near the front door, with my back to the wall, ready to start up the woeful ballad of the child who wanted to move like the others. I was confident, even blasé, and my attention drifted to two cats that were pulling each other's fur out in the garden. From my mouth came my usual chorus:

"I wanna move! I wanna move!"

From time to time I looked toward my father, who was rocking languorously to my singing. He got up to get the ashtray from the wardrobe. Suddenly he turned around and took three firm steps toward me. Quick as a flash he grabbed my arm, then both my ears.

"*Ti vous dinagi? J'vais ti douni di dinagima!* [Ya wanna move? I'll give ya move!]"

He spoke to me in French, and for about ten minutes he really did move me around house with his heavy hands and his size-nine boots. When he started beating me, I curled up in a ball to dull the pain, begging:

"No. No. Stop! Abboué. Stop! I don't wanna move any more."

"Oh, yes. Ya wanna move!"

"No, I don't want to any more."

"You're gonna move all right, I'm telling ya."

The pain became unbearable. Eventually my bruised body could fear no worse. Then hatred exploded in my head and knocked everything aside:

"Yes, wanna move! Yeah, I'm sick of being here. I wanna leave this rotten house. Let go of me! Let go of me!" I screamed.

Bouzid must have stopped listening to me some time ago, and he carried on with the punishment. Eventually I stopped screaming. He calmed down, then went back to his chair to finish his coffee, which must have gone cold. It was only then that my mother took me in her arms and carried me to my bed. I carried on with my demands as I passed my torturer:

"I wanna move!"

My mother, fearing that I'd get moved again, reassured me:

"Don't cry, son. We'll move."

"When?"

"Tomorrow morning."

"You're lying! It's not true. I wanna move now."

A few minutes later she brought me some semolina pancakes all covered in golden sugar. But I was already in the land of dreams, in the midst of moving house.

❨ ❨ ❨

The house was shrouded in darkness. Another quiet, uneventful evening was slipping away. Sitting on one of the kitchen steps, I was waiting for the hit parade to begin on the radio. Zohra was waiting too. I was waiting to hear Richard Anthony sing "Five Hundred Miles." "If you miss the train I'm on, you will know that I have gone. . . . Lord I'm five hundred miles away from home." I shivered. A fresh breeze glided past, stroking my cheeks, but not moving a single curl in my hair. I straightened my anorak.

My mother, busy in the kitchen, was preparing pasta with white sauce. Bouzid's eyes were fixed on her, but he seemed not to see her. He was no doubt listening to the announcer on Radio-Cairo or Radio-Algiers on his radio, but without understanding them.

The *quinquis* [oil lamps] were lit.

"Hey, come and see who's just arrived," called out Moustaf, racing into the yard.

We went straight out.

"Who is it?" asked Zohra, unable to make out the people who were sitting in the taxi.

"It's the Bouchaouis," I said.

I recognized them immediately.

"I'm gonna call Dad."

The head of the Bouchaoui clan got out of the car, paid the driver, and helped his wife pull her plump rear end through the door.

Some visitors, at last! It has been such a long time!

My father and my mother came out on the front steps.

"Bouchaoui," he cried, his arms wide open. "It's been such a long time. Why did you never come back to see us? Did you forget us or what? How are you? And the family? How's things? How are you?"

Bouzid was smiling radiantly. He was happy; his face was beaming. He kissed the former Chaâba resident, hugged him, and tapped him on the shoulder.

"And your children? They've really grown! Allah be praised!"

He kissed his wife, who was already telling my mother a thousand and one tales.

"But we are standing here talking, talking! Come into the house. Oh, what a pleasure to see you again. How are you?"

"We're fine!"

"How are you? And your children? And your wife?"

"Fine, Allah be praised!"

It was Saturday. We were going to have a happy night. I hopped and jumped for joy. I was like a dog with a bone, running around Zohra.

"Oh, stop it. You're crazy!" she shouted at me.

Coffee, cakes, even couscous! Yes, a huge couscous to celebrate the event. The Bouchaouis had come back to see us. Fortunately, my father had bought some lamb the previous day.

In the kitchen Yemma put on her apron, opened the drawers and cupboards, took out can openers, knives, her couscous steamer, and vegetables.

Yemma was happy, happier than she had been for months.

"As long as Louise doesn't come this evening," she whispered to Zohra. "Go to the door, go. If you see her coming, shut the gate. Go on, hurry up. Oh, my goodness, you're so slow, my girl!"

Zohra smiled, then went to station herself in front of the door. She knew that in a few minutes her mother would call her back to ask her to help peel the vegetables. She understood.

Madame Bouchaoui, embarrassed to find herself with the men, joined my mother in the kitchen.

"I'll help you, Messaouda!"

"No, there's no need. Stay where you are, please."

Madame Bouchaoui replied with a mischievous laugh:

"Do you want me to stay and talk with the men?"

Meanwhile my father was serving coffee to Bouchaoui, sprinkling it with plenty "How are you's?" The two men had already forgotten where they were. Engrossed in their tales, they were back in El-Ouricia, long ago.

Mother shook them out of their dreams when she called out:

"Come on, dinner's ready."

Zohra filled two large plates. One plate for the children and one for the two men, seated at the living room table. The women ate in the kitchen.

At our table Bouzid and Bouchaoui had already talked about a thousand and one things. Now that the euphoria of being together had subsided, they were talking about more serious things. It was Bouchaoui who started, as if the evening had been meticulously planned.

"I know that you are trying to leave this place, Bouzid."

My father pulled back immediately.

"What d'ya mean? Leave this place."

Bouchaoui interrupted him bluntly:

"Don't say no. I know very well how you've been living here since everybody left. It's miserable!"

"So you're just like them. Don't you realize that I'm at home here, I'm not disturbing anyone, and I don't owe anybody anything. I am happy here. Do you think I can find this elsewhere?"

This time my father's points were registered.

"All that is true, Bouzid. I would be lying if I said the opposite, but you have to admit that you have nothing here, no *litriziti* [electricity] . . ."

"I'll get it put in."

"How will you get the money?"

"I'll find it!"

"You don't even have tap water. Come and see my place, and you'll see what it's like to turn on a switch and have hot water. It's so convenient!"

With their ears pricked up like radio antennae, the women listened silently.

"Listen, Bouzid, I've found a flat for you in Lyon. All modern conveniences, close to mine. You'll be much better off than here. No, I can see in your eyes that you think I came here to talk you into it. No. Believe me, I don't want to force you. You are free. Come and see it, or don't. Do what you like. You know, I have nothing to gain."

As soon as he finished his speech, Bouchaoui, like an animal lapping up his drink, slurped up a big mouthful of curdled milk. The viscous liquid painted his fleshy lips white. My father chewed a piece of meat between his teeth, sucked the marrow, which he loved, and tapped the bone on the side of the table so that he could release its unctuous contents.

Moustaf turned toward me, trying to hide behind his spoonful of couscous.

"He's crafty, Bouchaoui. That's how to talk to father. He's going to get him."

I rubbed my hands with a malicious smile. My father saw my excitement and got angry.

"Go to bed, both of you. What are you listening to? Go on, git outta here!"

Moustaf took me by the sleeve and pulled me toward the bedroom. This wasn't a good time to be getting in the way.

About one o'clock in the morning the Bouchaouis left in spite of my father's pleas:

"You're mad, Bouchaoui! At this time of night you can't go home. You must sleep here."

"No, really, Bouzid, we're going home," the guest insisted.

Bouchaoui was determined to return to Lyon, and my father didn't insist, fearing that our guest didn't fancy spending the night in a house with so few conveniences.

"And how are you and the family going to get back?"

"By taxi."

"And where will you find a taxi? Are you going to telephone?"

"No, no. We'll walk to Villeurbanne, and we're sure

to find a taxi there. Don't worry about us, Bouzid. It's for the best."

"Are you going to walk all the way to Villeurbanne at one o'clock in the morning?"

"Yes, yes, don't worry. Come on, children, get your coats on."

My father felt bitter. He let Bouchaoui and his family leave, but only after accompanying them to the Avenue Monin, at the end of the embankment.

When he returned, I was still awake, and I heard him join my mother in bed. He spoke to her:

"Haven't you got anything to say?"

All evening she hadn't said a word, for fear of influencing him. His question took her by surprise.

"What do you want me to say?" she whispered. "You decide."

After some rustling of the sheets and creaking of the joints of the marital bed, the house fell silent again. It wasn't until long after my father had stopped whispering that I fell asleep, exhausted by the diabolical sound of his snoring.

❨ ❨ ❨

"Well, did you hear anything or not? What time did you fall asleep? What did they say?"

"What? Let me get back to sleep."

"Hey, are you going to wake up or not? I am talking to you."

Moustaf was anxious. He wanted to know the outcome of the previous evening's events.

"What did they say last night?"

"I don't know; let me get back to sleep."

"No! Not until you've given me an answer."

"Wednesday. On Wednesday Father's going to see a flat in town with Monsieur Bouchaoui."

I pulled the blanket up to my bare shoulders. But Moustaf suddenly went crazy, started doing standing jumps on the bed, hitting me with the pillow, shaking me, all the while continuing his interrogation.

"Are you sure? Tell me again what they said! Where are they going to meet on Wednesday?"

This time, I called for paternal assistance.

"Abboué! Abboué! Moustaf won't let me sleep."

He calmed down.

"Are you stupid or what, waking Dad up about this? If he gets up, we'll both be in for it."

He got up and disappeared somewhere. I couldn't sleep any more. With my eyes puffed up, my teeth clogged with bits of meat from the night before, and my ears buzzing, I extracted myself from under my blanket and went toward the kitchen, where Zohra was already making the coffee. I liked the smell of it on Sunday mornings. My father joined me. My argument with Moustaf had woken him up. His face showed no sign of emotion. Without looking at me he went to shave in the cool water of the pool. In the quiet of the morning we heard the thumping of the pump.

℃ ℃ ℃

It would soon be the end of June. The summer holidays. Happy at the thought of discovering a new life like Rabah, Hacène, and the Bouchaouis, but sad like an old man already lamenting the relics of his past, I looked at what was left of the dying Chaâba. Gone were the days of the embankment, the garbage trucks, the cabins in the forest, the hookers, Ma Louise, and school.

It was time to move on. Monsieur Grand was beginning to worry about my results. In the end-of-year compositions my work had suffered. For a while now my heart hadn't been in it.

"Passed and admitted to fifth grade."

Zohra translated for my father.

"He'll go to the big school now."

Bouzid was happy. But not excessively.

On the last day of the school year I left Léo-Lagrange without fully realizing that I would never pass through its gate again, that I would never again see Monsieur Grand.

At five o'clock Zohra and Moustaf were waiting for me at the main gate. We set off on our journey for the last time to return to what was left of Le Chaâba. Zohra was singing about being free.

"Give me your hand and take mine. School is out, and. . . ."

She'd heard the words on the hit parade.

"Bye, Léo-Lagrange! For ever," Moustaf cried, excited.

They started walking, bouncing with joy. I followed a few yards behind, dawdled across the Croix-Luizet canal bridge, which no longer scared me, strolled along under the plane trees on the boulevard, then entered the Avenue Monin. With a heavy heart I gazed at all the places I loved. At the prefabs I stopped for a minute to watch the gesticulations of a policeman directing the traffic. A few yards away I saw Moussaoui, the rebel.

Oh, he really had asked for his expulsion. Who knows, perhaps he'll become a good mechanic one day? I watched him disappear into the prefabs, with a brisk step, looking relaxed.

Zohra shouted to me to catch up.

"Are you coming then? What on earth are you looking at?"

"Nothing. I'm coming."

I ran to join her, surprised that the only thing she could think of was the holidays.

There, at the end of the track, was our house. My nostalgia faded away.

"Come on. Enjoy yourself," said Moustaf, giving me his usual pat on the back. "Just think, we're moving house."

I managed a slight smile.

❰ ❰ ❰

We moved house the first weekend of August 1966. In the back of the *Bijou* [Peugeot] 403 belonging to an Arab from El-Ouricia who worked with my father, we loaded an old metal bed, a wardrobe with a mirror, and all our clothes. My father wanted to take the stove. He did not believe in the *souffage satral* [central heating] in the new apartment in town. But he eventually gave in to pressure from the driver, who was more concerned about the wear and tear on his car than our personal problems. The stove was finally abandoned. It was destined to perish amid the cold walls of Bouzid's house in Le Chaâba.

I did not want to leave too quickly. I wanted to see, once more, the potholed yard, the cement-patched pool, which over the years had leaked like a sieve, the pump that had given us water from the Rhône for years, the deserted garden, the half-collapsing toilet. Everything.

Moustaf interrupted my thoughts abruptly:

"What're you doing? Do you want to stay here or what? You were crying because you wanted to move, and, now that we're leaving, you're dragging your heels. Come on, shut the door, we're going."

I could see he was right, and I ran to the car. I sat next to Zohra, just above the base of the bed. My mother was squeezed in on the floor of the Bijou, between Moustaf and me. The car followed the potholed lane that led to the boulevard and from there to the big city. For a long time we watched the house disappearing slowly by the side of the forest. Seated in the front passenger seat, Bouzid had not spoken for a long time. Mother was crying and smiling, holding the edge of her binouar between her fingers.

( ( (

"Oh, isn't it lovely!" Zohra burst out laughing as we entered the apartment.

"Right, OK, that's enough! Don't start opening your big mouth, you. You'll bring the evil eye on us," Yemma shot back.

My sister put her hand on her mouth to take back the words she had just let slip. Where we come from, *el-rhaïn* [the evil eye] was no joke. When Allah bestowed any kind of happiness on us, we should never boast about it to anyone, lest the devil interfere. Yemma had always said that.

From the entrance hall we gazed at the dreamworld for which we had so longed to leave Le Chaâba—a kitchen, a sitting room, and two little windowless alcoves. Mother suddenly sensed that I was watching her, so she went forward, took a few steps toward the kitchen furniture, and touched the wall coverings. What was she thinking about? About the farm in El-Ouricia where she had been a servant? About what she was going to do in her new home? Her face remained inscrutable. The minutes ticked by in silence. Then Zohra lost another marvelous opportunity to keep quiet when she turned to me and whispered:

"I'll sleep on the sofa. The sitting room will be my bedroom."

"You, you, you . . . ," said Yemma. "You'll go back to the *gourbi* [hovel] if you carry on like that!"

"I didn't say anything!" protested my sister.

"Go and undo a box then, instead of showing us your big teeth."

Sheepishly, Zohra picked up the first bag she could find under her feet and took it to the back of the kitchen, while Yemma returned to the staircase to help Staf, whose exasperated sighs could be heard from the distance. She said to me:

"Come and help us, you too."

"I'm coming, Yemma."

She went out. Zohra took advantage of her absence to call me back:

"Hey! Zouz. Look. There's the john and the washbasin over there."

From a hygiene point of view, this den was much

better than the one my father had dug in Le Chaâba, and there was even an automatic light inside. But something puzzled me. I asked my sister:

"Where does the poop go when you've done it?"

"It goes down the pipes. You see, the pipes on the walls of the building. And then it goes down all the way to the sewers," she replied.

"So there's no pool to empty here?"

"That's right. Everything here is modern."

"It's better than Le Chaâba," I said.

"Well, that's for sure!" replied Zohra.

"And where is the bathroom?"

We looked around us hoping to discover a little room in which the bath was hiding.

"There isn't one!" concluded my sister. "Fortunately, we've brought our green bathtub from Le Chaâba!"

At that moment Yemma came in, and I immediately said:

"Yemma!? Why does Zidouma's home have a bathroom but not ours?"

This time she flew into a wild rage, ran toward Zohra, grabbed her by her ponytail, and dragged her out of the toilet screaming:

"In the name of Allah! What did I do to deserve such a talkative witch?"

"It wasn't me! It wasn't me!" cried my sister. Then, hoping to save her skin, she pointed an accusing finger at me:

"It was him!"

I objected vigorously.

"What's the matter with her? Have you gone mad or something?"

Too late. Yemma turned her periscope toward me. She spun around like a lioness, looked for something to throw at me, and grumbled as she invoked Allah:

"Give me something, a hammer or a stone, so that I can smash this devil. Oh, Allah."

Finally, as usual she took off her shoe and threw it at me. As usual I had ample time to make myself scarce.

"*Artaille!*" she cursed, as she watched her shoe hit the wall.

❦ ❦ ❦

I nearly knocked Staf down the stairs. The poor guy had been as busy as a Turk all morning. Bouzid hadn't allow him a moment's rest. His arms were loaded with bags and boxes.

"Here. Take this!" he ordered me.

Then he asked:

"Well, what's it like?"

"Well, I don't think much of it. For a start it's very dark. When you open the window, all you see is the front of the building opposite. It'll never get any sun. And then it's very small. And there's no bathroom."

"OK, shut up!" he ordered me. "You're getting on my nerves. When we were in Le Chaâba, you were crying 'cos you wanted to move, and, now that we've moved, you're still crying."

"I'm not crying. And, besides, you asked me to tell you . . ."

He interrupted me:

"Take this, and shut it!"

"Well you can carry the boxes yourself if you want to be like that!"

So speaking, I deposited my load on a step and ran away.

"Come back, you stupid ass!" he screamed.

"You make me puke!" I said.

He let go of his load and pursued me furiously. I rushed down the stairs, three steps at a time, holding on to the rail for support. Suddenly, at a bend in the stairs, I crashed head-on into my father, who was dripping with sweat under the weight of an enormous mattress. His load fell over. My father too. Panic-stricken, I carried on racing down madly, hoping that he had not recognized me in the rush.

"Oh! Allah! *Zalouprix d'hallouf!* [You dirty pig!] Come here! Come here, I'm telling you. Now."

I made my way back up the steps slowly. Bouzid was now bright red. This time he was going to skin me alive. Staf emerged running out of nowhere. Even before he could see the full extent of the damage, I took advantage of his presence to get out of the fix:

"It's his fault, Abboué. I told him: 'Wait, I'll help carry your boxes.' He said: 'Get out of the way.' And then he told me he was fed up working. And he wanted to beat me so I would stay with him. He's mad."

Staf was stunned. He stood there with his mouth wide open. Bouzid unleashed his thunderous fury on him:

"*Zaloupard di Gran Bazar! Zalouprix di Mounouprix!* [You dirty pig! You filthy swine!] So, you're fed up with working, are you?! I'm going to pull your eyes out."

Staf tried to defend himself:

"Abboué, no. Abboué. It's not true. He's lying. *Ouallah* [in the name of Allah], he's lying. I swear on my father's life, he's lying."

Unruffled, Bouzid advanced toward him. My brother curled up like a hedgehog, protecting his head with his forearms. He was ready to take the blows. It served him right for bossing me about. Abandoning him to the boxing ring, I went out into the street.

( ( (

From the rue Terme I worked my way to the top of La Croix-Rousse by taking the *traboules* [narrow alleyways]. I crossed the roads beneath apartment blocks, climbed flights of steps, and passed through dark alleyways that smelled of pee. A lot of Arab families lived in the neighborhood.

It was about six o'clock. I had to return home. I headed back down to the Place Sathonay via the Montée de la Grande Côte. There were food shops, butchers, hairdressers, bars, hotels—it was like being in Algeria. Women, dressed like my mother, walked cheerfully across the road and entered the passageway opposite. In front of the shop windows Arabs with mustard yellow turbans, looking like old filter-tip cigarettes, stood sunning themselves.

On the staircase that led to our apartment not the slightest trace of our move remained. Dreamily I knocked on the door. It was opened with lightning speed. Staf's head appeared as if on a giant screen, and I found myself pinned up against the wall, immobilized by an armlock. My brother, using his legs as a weapon, kicked me over and over on my thighs to pay me back for the trick I'd played on him that afternoon with the unwitting help of my father. With his tongue between his teeth he threatened me, savoring my awkward posture:

"I told ya I'd get ya."

I called my father to the rescue:

"Abboué! Abboué! He's hitting me."

My brother became worried and tightened his grip.

"Shut up, or I'll beat you up for good."

I screamed even louder for help. He let go of me, but it was too late. Bouzid had heard my call. He went up to Staf and, without further ado, gave him a terrible kick in the butt before shouting at him:

"*Espèce de fainiaine* [you lazy-good-for-nothing], all you can do is beat your brother up. Aren't you ashamed? What kind of man are you?"

Completely crushed, Staf put both hands on his thighs to check they were still attached to his backside and retreated inside, crying with hatred and pain. All he dared say was:

"I'm sick of it. It's always me who gets it."

Then he stared at me:

"You'll see, one of these days I'll smash your teeth!"

Hiding behind my father, I pulled a long, sneering face at him to make him even more furious. He cried for a few moments on his mattress. Then he took one of my books and switched on the light for it was already dark at home and in the alcoves it was pitch black. My father returned to the charge:

"Switch off that light! Do you want to bankrupt me

now or what? You don't have to pay for the litriziti."

Staf's exasperation redoubled.

Then Bouzid turned toward Yemma and said almost as gruffly:

"So? Isn't it ready yet?"

In the kitchen Yemma was kneading the semolina dough to make some galettes. She didn't look happy. But she continued working, moving around the brand-new, bright blue Formica furniture that the previous tenant had sold to my father, along with the television, a bed with a padded headboard, and a sofa, all for a price that Bouchaoui had judged to be a bargain.

Staf was still groaning in his alcove. Pitying him, Zohra turned against me.

"This is all your fault, you damn fool."

I walked up to her nonchalantly, and, as soon as she turned her head toward me, I landed a neat uppercut on her face. My fist fell on her eye. She screamed:

"Ouch! Ouch! My eye! I can see electricity in my eye. I've gone blind. Abboué, I'm blind."

"What's that about litriziti? Switch everything off. Oh, you gang of devils, sons of demons, impure heathens, Jews, you'll be the death of me. Get out, *digage dlà* [get out of here], all of you. Get to bed, all of you."

That was how the evening ended. Mother cooked only one galette and offered it to the old man. He said he wasn't hungry any more. Then they went to sleep in their padded bed.

( ( (

Every morning Yemma would tidy her new *bart'mâ* [apartment]. She seemed to enjoy cleaning the tiled floor, which was as smooth as the windowpanes. She spent hours on end polishing the table, the chairs, and the Formica wall cupboards. She was fascinated by all the new objects around her. Look at the way she caressed the fridge as she cleaned it. She was afraid of scratching it.

When my mother was happy, I felt good. The apartment was joyful and welcoming. Almost bright. While Bouzid was out at work, Yemma was queen of the castle, relaxed. One day Zohra was teaching her how to use the electric iron. I took advantage of the old man's absence to watch the television. Yemma was worried that he would see an unusual increase in the electricity bill.

"Please, my son, switch it off; if not, he'll end up smashing it one day," she said.

"Oh, no, Yemma. I'm just going to watch a little. Just the film, then I'll switch it off. OK?"

She did not answer. I took this as a sign that she had given in.

Almost at the same moment there was a knock on the door.

"My God, it's your father. Quick, switch off the *tilifiziou* [television]!" she begged me.

I obeyed immediately and followed her into the hall. It couldn't be my father since he was at work. Suddenly I was scared that something dreadful might have happened. Yemma was shaking all over. She walked to the door, and, looking with terror-stricken eyes at every corner of the room as if she were looking for something, she said a prayer to Allah. With her hand on the door handle she asked:

"*Chkoun?* [Who is it?]"

"Open the door. Are you scared?" a woman's voice replied.

"*Chkoun?*" she repeated.

"Don't tell me you don't recognize me?" replied the mysterious voice.

It was a very familiar voice. Suddenly Yemma's eyes lit up, and she cried:

"Oh, Zidouma!"

She threw open the door, threw her arms around Zidouma, kissed her four times, mumbled some of the usual greetings, and invited her in.

"*Gharbi, gharbi* [Welcome, welcome]," she said, overcome with emotion.

Zidouma was also happy to see her again. After the bloody fights that had taken place in Le Chaâba toward the end, I had thought that we would never again see the burly frame of Zidouma. And here she was, more plump that ever, flashing her big teeth with their gold crowns, as if the two women had always been the best of friends. Then, taking out of her wicker basket a packet of sugar and a packet of coffee, the essential calling cards of a North African visitor, she crossed our threshold and immediately started saying:

"Oh, isn't this lovely, and this too. *Hou là là* [goodness me], you are lucky. Good for you. Good."

Her eyes greedily took in the wall coverings, the two pictures hanging on the wall, the Formica furniture, the fridge, and the cooker.

"The tenant who used to live here left all these things," mother explained.

Under normal circumstances, she would have certainly thought that hidden somewhere in Zidouma's exuberance was an evil eye, which would have had her running straight for a *marabout* [holy man]. But today there was no rhaïn, no *mrabta* [holy woman]. She was overjoyed because she had a bart'mâ just like Zidouma and because there was no need to envy her any more. While Mother pointed out all the ins and outs—"Here's the Formica *blouc* [countertop], the table and chairs that the old tenant left behind, along with the bed and the padded headboard"—Zidouma expressed her admiration with repeated *Oh!*'s.

I switched the TV back on while the two women chatted more and more loudly, as if they were in the marketplace. When my mother said she was worried she might not meet any Arab neighbors at the market, Zidouma informed her that the Saadis, who used to live in Le Chaâba, were among our neighbors. She gave her their address, which was in her bag.

"I'll go and see them tomorrow," said mother. "It isn't nice living by yourself."

I could not hear the television any more, so I got up to turn up the volume, but Yemma got annoyed and told me to go to the devil. I told her I'd rather watch the film, so she walked straight up to the television and unplugged it.

"I'll switch it back on anyway," I said.

Zidouma interrupted in her loud voice:

"Are you going to let us chat in peace? Go and enjoy yourself outside; it's nice out there!"

"I don't have any friends here."

"Well, go and find some!" she said. "Go and find Ali Saadi; he knows everyone here."

My mother followed on:

"Yes, go on, my son. Tell his mother that I'll be coming to see them tomorrow. Go on, my son. Be a good boy."

I resigned myself to going out. It wasn't every day that my poor mother had a chance to chat like this.

( ( (

The neighborhood was dead, stifled by the heat beating down on the fronts of the apartment blocks. From time to time an occasional car or bus disturbed the silence.

Two old men dawdling along the road in the baking heat went past me without looking at me. I walked toward the Place Bellecour. All the store windows were shut. "Will reopen on September 3." "Annual holiday closure." What was there to do in this desert? I returned home. I would go to see Ali another time.

At the entrance to our alleyway Yemma and Zidouma were exchanging a few last words. My mother had forgotten that we were no longer in Le Chaâba. She stood there, entirely at ease in her binouar, right in the middle of the road. Zidouma, for her part, was wearing a fashionable pleated skirt and stiletto heels. If she hadn't been so plump, you could have taken her for a native. The two women exchanged kisses. Zidouma went off toward the bus stop for the Villeurbanne bus. I watched her disappear at the end of the road. I would have preferred to live near them and see Hacène and Rabah everyday, as we used to in Le Chaâba. Here times were going to be hard for us. Mother could already feel it as she waved a last good-bye.

❨ ❨ ❨

At the end of the rue Terme, Bouzid came round the corner, slumped on his moped, suffocating in the heat. I waited for him at the edge of the sidewalk. Yemma had gone back in. He came up to me, got off his motor, pushed it into the alleyway, mechanically, while asking me in a neutral tone:

"What are you doing here?"

I told him I wasn't doing anything in particular.

When he reached the courtyard, he leaned his moped against the wall and took out of the saddlebags the tin from which he'd eaten his lunch, then walked heavily toward the staircase. It was only then that I greeted him with a kiss. I was worried by the protruding bones of his cheek, which for some time now had been getting more and more hollow. Old Bouzid had lost a lot of weight. His face looked drawn, and I felt distant from him.

Only two weeks earlier he had spent a lot of money buying furniture that he could have happily done without, paying a three months' advance to the apartment manager, paying for the documents and the move itself. That evening he had gotten an advance on his wages. Seated at the table, he examined his receipt, deciphered it, not knowing in which direction to hold the paper, then, finally, as usual, asked me to help him:

"Come and read this to me! How much did they write?"

I took the paper, holding it the correct way up, and

looked for the box where the answer had been written.

"Thirty-three thousand francs, Abboué."

"Thirty-three thousand francs," he repeated, then fell silent.

And there he was, lost again in his obscure calculations, his pay slip in his hand and his eyes half closed, a sign that he was thinking very hard. He counted, thought ahead, planned, and counted again. With his finger he drew imaginary figures on the table.

Just opposite him Yemma was preparing dinner. Silently. She had not said a word to him since his arrival. She hadn't so much as looked at him. But she was keenly aware of his presence, without the need to look at him.

"Thirty-three thousand . . . twelve thousand . . . ," he repeated.

Then he called me.

"Come here; you're not doing anything."

"*Ouaiche* [what is it], Abboué?"

"Go and get me two tins of chemma from the tobacconist."

He gave me some coins. I took them, and suddenly a practical question came to my mind:

"How do you say *chemma* in French, Abboué?"

"*Tababrisi!* Ask for *tababrisi*."

I went down to the tobacconist in the Place Sathonay. He did not have any tababrisi. In fact he had never heard of such a product. I explained to him that it was the powder that people put in their mouth to smoke; then he raised his arms to the sky and said:

"You mean *tabac à priser* [chewing tobacco]?"

"Yes, two tins. And a packet of cigarette paper."

The tobacconist served me, laughing.

( ( (

The summer holidays were coming to an end. The neighborhood suddenly reawakened. There were more people in the streets, in the squares, and in the stores. Car horns could be heard echoing through the passageways between the apartment blocks. A strange hubbub.

In the Place Sathonay kids had been playing football the last few afternoons. The previous day Staf and I had watched them for a long time. Secretly we were waiting for one of them to come up to us and say:

"Do you want to play with us?"

None of them did. We returned home to watch the serial on TV.

( ( (

"Come on. Wake up. Time for *l'icoule* [school]," Yemma insisted, hammering me on my shoulder.

"What time is it?"

"A quarter to eight. Look, your brothers and sisters are ready to leave."

"Leave him," said Staf. "We're going."

"Go on then!" I said. "I don't care."

What a terrible feeling, putting on my Sunday best to go to school, to show the schoolmistress we were clean. The smell of the plastic school satchel, the eraser, the pencil case, and the exercise book covers all made me feel bitter.

I got up without enthusiasm, put on my gentleman's outfit, and sat down at the breakfast table.

"You can drink your milk tomorrow morning," screamed my mother. "Comb your hair and go."

Before leaving I grabbed a piece of galette that had been left on the cooker.

"Come on. Run along," said my mother, closing the door behind me.

The Ecole Sergent-Blandan [Sergeant Blandan School] was at the end of the road bearing the same name, two hundred yards from home. On the sidewalk, some boys and girls, their satchels in their hands, were walking sadly in the same direction. Here there was not the same eagerness as on school mornings at Le Chaâba. The children here went to school like the grown-ups went to work. There were no hookers, no bridge to cross on the way there, and, at the gate, the pupils, accompanied by their mothers, waited quietly for the bell to ring. No one here had heard of king and queen marbles!

"There you are at last," Staf shouted, happy at last to have someone to speak to.

As I went up to him, somebody came up behind me, put his hands over my eyes, and said:

"Guess who?"

Without allowing the stranger time to repeat his question, I turned around straight away, intrigued by this strange familiarity.

"Ali! You scared me," I said, full of surprise.

"What on earth are you doing here?" he asked.

"Well we live here now. Look, my brother's here too. We go to this school. I'm in fifth grade. What about you?"

"I am in sixth grade. But tell me, why didn't you come and see me at home? I live in the rue de la Vieille. It's just around the corner."

"We didn't know you were there. I'm glad I've met you here. You know, we're all alone here. We don't know anyone."

He smiled and interrupted me:

"That won't be a problem."

The bell rang. He concluded hurriedly:

"Damn, the bell is already ringing. Listen, we'll meet at the exit this evening because this afternoon I have to go with my mother to fill out some papers at the town hall. OK?"

"OK!"

Before entering the boys' playground I spotted Zohra at the girls' entrance. She was timidly watching a group of happy-looking pupils. I felt a little sorry for her. Catching my eye, she waved her hand in encouragement. I did the same.

Ali and Staf disappeared in the crowd, while a woman's voice called out in the playground:

"Fifth-grade pupils, this way!"

It was Madame Valard, my new teacher. Dressed in a rather unbecoming green blouse, she looked unfriendly with her little round glasses and her thin lips.

"Come on, follow me," she said, when we were all gathered behind her.

We settled into our classroom, with the teacher behind her desk. As she looked over the rows she said:

"I can see that I know a lot of you already. We were together last year."

Then, turning her eyes to the desk to my right:

"I see that Alain Taboul still can't separate himself from his brother."

The two aforementioned, whom I had taken to be compatriots for their skin was so dark and their hair so frizzy, smiled stupidly. With names like that they couldn't be Arabs.

The teacher went on:

"Have we a new pupil as well?!"

She stared at me. From the rows of desks, all heads turned with great curiosity toward me.

Madame Valard was holding my school report, no doubt sent by Monsieur Grand with details of my pedigree.

She said very loudly:

"Ho! Ho! We have a little genius with us!"

I looked down, and she spoke about something else. I felt uncomfortable.

( ( (

"So? How did it go today?" asked Ali, who had come to meet me at the exit. "D'you know that you are in the same class as my buddy Babar?!"

"No, I didn't know that. I told you this morning, I don't know anyone round here."

"Look!" carried on Ali. "There's Babar."

He introduced me.

"This is my cousin Azouz. We used to live together before."

"I saw you in class," said Babar.

I tried to explain:

"I don't know anyone yet."

He went on:

"I could see that. And I saw the teacher having a dig at you. Watch out; she's a bitch. She can't stand me; I don't know why. She says I'm a phony, but I don't understand why she says that because we don't have a phone."

Ali interrupted:

"If she really pisses you off, tell me. I'll do in all the wheels on her car. I know which one it is."

Babar laughed and concluded:

"Tomorrow I'll sit next to you."

I told him I liked the idea.

"What are you gonna stick your dick into now?" Ali asked.

"What am I what?" I said, surprised.

"I mean what are you up to?"

"I'm going home. I have to because my brother's already back home and I have to return with him; otherwise my father will skin me alive."

"Right, we'll come with you; that way you can show us where you crash."

I looked puzzled. Ali explained:

"He means where you live, you know. Holy shit, where did you learn to talk?"

He and Babar gently mocked my ignorance.

"Are your mom and dad ok?" asked my cousin.

"Yeah," I said. "*Kouci kouça.* [So-so.] My father didn't want to leave Le Chaâba, you know. Now, he misses it."

"We're better off than in the Chaâba shacks; you'll see. You just need to get used to it."

Babar added further encouragement:

"You'll get to know all our buddies. That way you won't be lonely."

Little by little I found myself feeling better and better. No more being on my own; no more watching television all day. As we went up the rue Sergent-Blandan we passed several gones that Babar and Ali knew. They introduced me. I was proud of being Ali's cousin. And, when they introduced me to Martine, I blushed a little. Ali seemed very much at ease with the girls, much more so than Babar. When Martine went off behind us, he even confided to me:

"She's been following me around for a long time, that one. D'you like her?"

I replied that her blonde hair was marvelous.

He said:

"Is that all?"

When we got home, Ali kissed my parents and held out his hand to my sister, as was customary with a young lady. Babar didn't want to come in. He said:

"I will wait out here."

Then my father went and brought him in, saying:

"*Atre! Atre boire café. T'en as pas peur?* [Come in! Come in, and have a coffee. You're not afraid?]"

Very embarrassed, Babar joined us, while we laughed at my father's accent.

We did not stay long. Ali and Babar said good-bye, and we went out into the street again.

"You see, that's the rue de la Vieille over there. It's not far," said Ali.

The road in question was indeed only a short distance from school. It looked like all the others with its paving stones, its gray walls and traboules. Outside number 3, we met a gone, sitting on the sidewalk, who didn't seem to be waiting for anything in particular.

"This is Kamel," said Ali.

I held out my hand to him, and he asked me:

"Where are you from in Algeria?"

"Sétif, and you?"

"Oran."

We spoke together like two friends who had known each other for years, and other kids came to join us as the red September sun went down behind the river Saône.

It was pitch black when I realized that Bouzid was waiting for me at home. So, drunk with joy, I ran down the streets from one pavement to the next, not for fear of being skinned alive, but because I was now a real gone.

At home Bouzid was waiting for me, not in the slightest degree drunk with joy:

"Where have you been, *zalouprix* [you swine]?" he screamed.

Sure of myself, I answered:

"With Ali, Abboué. I told you earlier that I was going to his house."

"That's it now, hallouf; you're starting to hang around the streets!"

I tried to divert the conversation by speaking to my mother:

"Yemma, Ali's mother says to say hello."

She said:

"Come, come and eat your dinner, my son!"

The Indian war chief cut in, shouting:

"Eat? Eat? No food for him this evening. He can eat outside with his street friends. If he's going to start coming in at eight o'clock, when he hasn't even got hair on his chin, what's he going to get up to next?"

Then, turning toward me:

"*Allez, fout'-moi l'camp da l'alcoufe! Halloul!* [Get the hell out of that alcove! You pig!]"

⟨ ⟨ ⟨

"Are you an Arab or a Jew?" the eldest of the Taboul brothers asked me while we were at break.

It was the first time he had spoken to me directly since school had started again. His brother was hanging around him as usual. If Babar had been with me, I would not have been scared of them. But he had not come to school that morning, and I felt vulnerable in the face of Madame Valard and now the Taboul brothers.

The moment that terrible question was asked, I had enough time, in a fraction of a second, to see the thousand and one consequences that my answer would have. I mustn't give the impression that I was hesitating.

"I am a Jew," I said with conviction.

The two Taboul brothers expressed their satisfaction. I knew that they were Jewish because, on television, all you could hear was news of the Six-Day War between the Arabs and the Israelis. That's why the eldest one frequently called his brother a *dirty Arab* when he wanted to hurl the vilest of insults at him. It was like Bouzid when he called one of us a *Jew*, a term he didn't bother to qualify as *dirty* since that went without saying.

I was a Jew, I said. Because there were two of them, the Tabouls, and because they knew the teacher and a lot of other pupils well. If I had admitted that I was an Arab, everybody would have frozen me out, apart from Babar, of course. And then the Tabouls also trotted out the fact that, in the desert, over there, a million Israelis had routed out several million Arabs, and I felt humiliated inside. So it was better for me to be Jewish.

"Why are you called Azouz?" asked Alain, puzzled by this Berber-sounding name.

"It's because my parents were born in Algeria, that's all. So my name comes from over there. But I was born in Lyon, so I am French."

"Oh, really?" said Alain, confused.

Fortunately I was saved by the bell. The bell called us back to work, but things did not look too good for the following days.

❨ ❨ ❨

It happened one evening at about five o'clock, when Madame Valard had just released us. I was going down the stairs that led directly to the sidewalk and the street, with my two fellow Jews at my side. Several moms were waiting for their kids. Suddenly a terrible vision loomed in the doorway. There, on the sidewalk, obvious for all to see in the middle of the other women, her binouar draped down to her heels, her hair hidden under a green head scarf, the tattoo on her forehead even more visible than usual, stood Yemma. There was no way to pass her off as Jewish and still less as French. She waved to catch my attention, at which point Alain said to his brother:

"Look, that Arab woman is calling you."

The brother burst out laughing in a vile way before continuing:

"Is that your wife?"

And they roared with laughter all the more. I stood there speechless, stranded like some Egyptian in the Sinai desert. I pretended to be tying my shoelaces so that I could wait for them to move away. And, when they had turned their backs to me, I gesticulated wildly and coldly at my mother! Using my eyes, my hands, every part of my body, I begged her to go away, to stand somewhere else. At first she did not understand my gestures at all and continued to smile and wave in my direction. Then, as my angry movements became more and more apparent, her smile disappeared from her lips, her arms fell to her side, and her body froze. Finally, she backed off and went to hide behind a car. I was saved! Meanwhile other moms were meeting their children with big hugs and kisses.

"Bye! See you tomorrow," said the Tabouls.

"See you later," Babar said to me. "In rue de la Vieille!"

"No! Wait for me!" I said to him. "I'm coming with you."

Yemma was still waiting for her son behind the car. I cast a glance toward her. The poor woman stood motionless. She saw me walk in the opposite direction from her and finally understood that I did not want to see her at all. So she walked off alone down the rue Sergent-Blandan to return home.

"See ya," I said to Babar. "I've decided to go home after all."

He didn't understand. I ran toward Yemma and caught up with her in two strides:

"Why did you wait for me in front of the school?" I asked her bluntly.

"To give you your snack. Look, I bought you *une briouche avec li chicoulat* [a chocolate bun]. Do you want it?"

She delicately took out the bun from one of her pockets.

"No, I don't want it. I'm not hungry, and, besides, I don't want you to come and wait for me in front of the school any more."

My violent outburst seemed to surprise her; then she asked sadly:

"Why?"

"I'm not a baby. I'm big enough to return home on my own."

"I won't come back to school again to bring your snack, my son. Don't be angry with me."

We walked for a few yards next to each other, and then she stopped, looked me straight in the eyes, and said:

"You're ashamed of me, aren't you?"

I said:

"Don't be stupid. What are you talking about?"

"I don't like it when you shout like that. Look! Everybody is looking at us."

"Why do you say I'm ashamed of you?"

"Because I don't look French, and because of my binouar."

I interrupted her:

"Oh, no, that's not it. I told you I don't want you to come and wait for me at the exit as if I was a baby. Look at my classmates: no one comes to wait for them!"

"Yes, yes, you're right, she said to me. It's my fault; I wanted to come out for some fresh air, and I thought I would buy you a snack and bring it to you at l'icoule."

"Give it to me now, Yemma. I'm hungry."

She gave me the chocolate bun, and we walked home. A deep feeling of humiliation took away my appetite.

❬ ❬ ❬

When Madame Valard gave out the results, she took pleasure in lingering over them, the cow!

"Azouz, seventeenth out of thirty. Not that good for a little ex-genius."

And then, to make my disgrace worse, I burst out crying in the middle of the class. She added:

"So you'd gotten used to being first, had you?!"

❬ ❬ ❬

At home my father said that I was no longer working at school because I was too busy hanging around with good-for-nothings in the street, instead of reading books like I used to in Le Chaâba. He refused to understand that it was Madame Valard's fault that I was seventeenth in the class. So I went off to the rue de la Vieille, and too bad if I got into trouble on my return.

Kamel was repairing the rear wheel of his bike.

"Hi, Kamel!"

"Hi. You ok?"

"Fine. You on your own?"

"Yeah," he replied. "But I'm expecting the others.

We're going for a bike ride out to where the farmers are. Do you want to come?"

"On what? I don't have a *braque* [bike]."

"Oh, you don't have any wheels?" he said, surprised.

Then he immediately added:

"Do you want one?"

"How do you mean, do I want one? Have you got one to pass on to me?"

"Don't fret about it. I'll finish repairing this bitch of a wheel; then we'll go and find you one."

A few minutes later we were on our way, heading for the Place Sathonay. The streets were deserted at that time of day. People were eating lunch.

"What are you going to do, Kamel?"

"We're gonna lift a braque for you. D'you want one or not?"

"Yeah. Of course, I want one. But I'm not into lifting stuff."

He burst out laughing.

"Me neither. You're going to lift it, not me. I'm going to keep a lookout. That's all."

We went up to the center of the square, at the foot of Sergeant Blandan's statue, where several bikes and mopeds were parked. Casually Kamel pointed to a magnificent red roadster.

"That one!" he said. "Go ahead. I'm watching."

"But what about the padlock? How do I get it off?"

He started getting annoyed at my hesitation.

"It's easy. You take the padlock like this. You turn it between your fingers, and it breaks open. Those things are no damn good. You'll see."

"I can't."

"You scared?"

"You bet."

"All right, let's get outta here," he concluded.

I hesitated a moment longer.

"No. Wait a bit; I'm going to do it."

"Good. Well, get a move on; otherwise someone will see us."

He moved a few steps away, turned his back to me, and looked around. The fear of stealing knotted up my stomach, and a terrible trembling shook my fingers. I couldn't feel my legs under me. I grabbed the padlock in my hand and twisted it in all directions. The bike fell to the ground with a crash. Kamel turned around.

"What the hell are you doing?" he asked, laughing.

"I can't break it."

"Press harder!"

I increased my pressure. Two spokes buckled in, and the lock finally broke.

"Got it, Kamel!"

Running like a madman through the square, I leaped onto the bike while Kamel jumped on the saddlebag.

"Pedal faster!" he shouted. "There's a guy running after us!"

I couldn't go any faster. My muscles were frozen.

"Where is he?" I said, turning around.

Kamel roared with laughter.

"Just kidding. You were really scared, weren't you?"

"You're stupid, making jokes like that."

"Come on, keep on riding! You see how easy it is to lift stuff."

We got to the rue Sergent-Blandan. I plunged into the central courtyard of my alleyway. I was safe! In no time at all the red bike became black. Private property.

"Come on then! Let's get back to the rue de la Vieille. And, while I remember, you'll have to pay for a new padlock."

"Yeah," I said. "It would be stupid to have someone steal it."

( ( (

"It serves you right: you wanted to leave. Well now you can dig yourselves out of the crap without me!"

During the several months that we'd been living here, this had become a ritual threat in the old man's mouth each time a problem arose at home. The previous week had been terrible. He did not give a single franc to my mother, and he even pocketed all the money from the family allowance, for fear we might waste it. The only thing we bought at the grocer's was milk, and mother cooked semolina bread every day to save money. The previous evening, when he got back from work, he had threatened cruelly:

"Not long now till I go back to Le Chaâba. Anyone who wants to eat will have to follow me."

And he left a few minutes later. We watched him grab a plastic bag, stuff some clothes and food in it, and leave without a single word for a pilgrimage to Le Chaâba. Yemma, impassive, did not cry. No doubt because she knew he'd be back in a few days. She was in fact relaxed after his departure, and so were we. As she closed the door behind him she had even shouted:

"Why don't you go and stew in your filthy Chaâba, you bum!"

As expected, he returned on Saturday. He opened the door very noisily, no doubt to alert us to his arrival, then came straight into the lounge. Huddled together around my mother, we were watching television, sitting on the sofa. None of us moved. The seconds seemed to last forever. Then a barely perceptible smile appeared on his lips, and a glimmer lit his eyes. He continued to stare at us, his bag in his hand, and we were stunned by his attitude. Yemma still did not look at him. He started smiling, then laughed out loud, as if his departure from home had been only a game. Zohra started chuckling first, then we all followed, and Yemma joined in last:

"So? You didn't starve? You can do without me easily," he said.

No one answered. Then he turned to Zohra:

"Right, go and make me a coffee."

She obeyed without saying a word.

If it had not been for that obscene kiss on the television, we would most certainly have spent a very pleasant evening. But there you are; that pig of an actor wanted to touch the girl's tongue, in front of us all, and that was something Bouzid couldn't stand. He lost his temper again:

"Switch off that filth! We're not in the street here?!"

None of us moved, so he rushed to the TV and pressed a button at random: it was the volume; then a second: it was the contrast; then a third: it was the tone. Then, in a fit of rage, he pulled the wire out of the socket and blew every fuse in the apartment. We were in total darkness, and the situation was pretty comic. Staf started cracking jokes.

"Go and find some candles instead of laughing, hallouf!" father howled.

"There aren't any," said Yemma, who had remained silent until then.

"Too bad then. We'll save on the litriziti. I don't want anyone switching on the tilifiziou any more. Do you understand? In fact I'm going to sell it."

Staf came up to me, anxious:

"Father's gone mad," he said.

I didn't know what to say. My father's sudden mood change certainly hadn't surprised me. Zohra joined us to add her two cents' worth:

"We can't even switch on the electricity when it's dark. We mustn't flush the toilet until it's been used several times. We mustn't switch on the television. He really is becoming a pain!"

"I'll be glad when he goes back to Le Chaâba for good," said Staf.

The following weekend Bouzid returned to Le Chaâba once again. To look after the garden, or so he said. Oh, yeah, to look after the garden!

❨ ❨ ❨

June that year was a tough month for me to get through at the Ecole Sergent-Blandan.

The schoolmistress had organized a parents' meeting on a Saturday to discuss the year's results.

She handed each of us a form for our parents to sign. I left mine in my school satchel. If I had given it to my father, he would have asked a lot of questions and in-

sisted on attending the parents' meeting. I did not want
him to miss work for such a small matter. And, if he
had, what would he have made of it? What would he
have said to the teacher? He would have listened to her
like a deaf person, pretending to understand by nodding his head. Madame Valard would soon have seen
how things were with him. I did not want my father to
be seen in that light.

She kept me back one evening after class. She asked
me about my parents' absence, and I replied that my
father worked on Saturdays.

"And your mother?" she went on.

I said she was ill, but the teacher didn't seem to believe me at all. It was the first time she'd spoken in a
way that didn't give me the creeps. She asked me about
my family. I told her that my father was a construction worker and my mother did nothing. She asked
me at what age I had arrived from Algeria, and I then
pointed out to her proudly that I was born in Lyon,
in the city's largest hospital: Grache-Blache [Grange-
Blanche], as Yemma and Abboué used to say. Then,
smiling, she asked me if I was happy to be moving
up to the lycée [high school]. I replied that Monsieur
Grand, my teacher at Léo-Lagrange, had always told
me that I would be good enough to go on to the lycée.
She laughed, thinking I was overconfident, but I left the
classroom feeling that I'd won a major battle.

The Taboul brothers were waiting for me in the
street.

"So? What did she say?" asked the eldest.

The other one followed on:

"Are you going on to high school? Which one?"

I replied simply:

"The Lycée Saint-Exupéry."

When the eldest informed me that their parents had decided to send them to a private school full of priests, I was overwhelmed with joy. Ever since the Tabouls had forced me to swap the Koran for the Torah, I cursed myself each time I was in their company.

Before we separated they wanted me to go up to their house. I said that my mother was waiting for me at home. And, as I left them, I shouted out a "*Salam oua rlikoum*" with a typical southern French accent. They both burst out laughing and said I could almost pass for an Arab. I laughed too.

( ( (

My father was already back from work when I returned home. I announced to him calmly:

"Abboué, I'm moving up to seventh grade."

He congratulated me; then, puzzled by *seventh grade*, he turned toward Zohra and said:

"What's *seventh grade*?"

She replied:

"It's *la grande icoule* [the lycée]."

He promised to take me to the flea market on Sunday. I asked him for permission to watch the television: granted!

( ( (

The Lycée Saint-Exupéry was situated in a different part of La Croix-Rousse, a quarter of an hour from home. On the first day of the school year, as I stood waiting for the bus to school, anguish and excitement battled with each other in my head. The previous evening Yemma had scrubbed me as clean as her fridge, in the green tub. My skin was white. The other pupils waiting for the bus with me looked at me from time to time, sheepishly, shy and just as white as I was.

The front of the bus appeared round a sharp bend in the rue Terme. It wasn't going to "Croix-Rousse Cemetery." It was the wrong bus. A pupil got on, and the doors shut behind him. Surprised, he noticed, as the bus moved off, that no one had followed him. He would arrive late.

A few minutes later, the "Cemetery" bus appeared, crammed with people. With a screeching loud enough to split one's ears, its gigantic wheels braked, and it came to a halt just where I was standing. I got ready to jump on. An old lady seized my satchel, pulled it back, and swore at me:

"What bad manners. Can't you see that I'm old!"

I let her get on before me, then readied myself again to jump on.

"Full up! The bus is full up! Take the next one, it's coming," shouted the conductor.

I took two steps back, confused. Fortunately a loud burst on a horn announced the arrival of the next bus. It was full of pupils, heading no doubt for the Lycée Saint-Exupéry. The bus struggled up to the top of La Croix-Rousse.

"Rue Hénon!" shouted the driver.

The stream of satchels got off. I joined the flow.

The lycée was just opposite the bus stop. It looked majestic. I was walking on my own, near three pupils who seemed to have known each other for a long time and who were telling each other about their holidays. I went into the huge central playground with them. Dozens of pupils were jostling each other in front of the lists posted on the walls. One of them screamed:

"Fantastic! We are together."

The others, like me, said nothing. Doing my best to look casual about it so that others would not pity me, I looked for my name. There! Class 7B, room 110. I glanced at the names that followed. There were no compatriots in 7B. I looked behind me into the playground, where hundreds of pupils were waiting for the bell. In the distance, looking at the last list of names, I saw a "frizzy hair." He saw me too, stared at me for a minute, then looked away. He must have been lost like me, poor guy. He looked at me again, and I gave him a barely perceptible nod. He responded in an equally imperceptible manner.

The eight o'clock bell rang. The pupils who had been all over the playground now lined up in front of the pillars. The whole of 7B was now gathered together. Suddenly I started dreaming about Le Chaâba, Léo-Lagrange, all the kids I used to meet in the morning at the gate, the way they would say: "Hi! Come and stake your king marble!" and how rich I had felt then while we were waiting for the janitor to open the gate. A feeling of nostalgia tugged at my heart. While we were lining up, furtive glances met and clashed. I didn't know where to look. I stared at the list of names, which I had already looked at a thousand times. The headmaster appeared and said we were now going to have to start working seriously; then he invited us to join our classes and teachers. I really wanted to return to Monsieur Grand's class!

❰ ❰ ❰

"Do you know where our classroom is?" a pupil asked me as we went up the stairs.

"No," I said to him. "I'm new to this school."

"Me too," he continued. "Where are you from?"

I was a bit surprised by the question, but I answered quickly:

"I was born in Lyon."

"No, I mean which school were you at last year?"

"Oh! Which school? Sergent-Blandan. It's very close to the Place des Terreaux."

"Don't know it," said the pupil. "I was in Paris before; then my parents moved to Lyon."

"Oh!" I said, pretending to be surprised.

He went on:

"My name's Alain. What's yours?"

"Begag," I said, carrying on walking.

"Do you have any friends in this school?"

"Yeah, of course. I have lots, but they're not in the same class as us."

"Well, I don't know anyone. Could I sit next to you?"

"If you like."

A glimmer of hope appeared in his eyes. "Another lost soul," I said to myself. "Like me." We reached room 110 after walking along an endless corridor. It was open, but the class teacher was not there. A few pupils went in. I followed them in with the lost Parisian.

"Where shall we sit?" he asked me.

The front rows had been left empty by those who had already settled in.

"Listen," I said, "we can just sit in the second row."

"That'll suit me because I can't see anything with my glasses."

A little later the teacher burst into the classroom; his eyes took in each of our faces at a glance; he closed the door behind him, greeted us with a smile, and sat down at his desk, which was raised on a platform. He stared at the groups of pupils who had positioned themselves at the back of the class and said to them:

"Do I scare you? Come and sit in the front row."

Everybody obeyed, and two pupils came to sit just in front of our desk.

"Aren't you better there?" the teacher said ironically.

"Yes, yes, M'sieur," replied one of them, believing that the question was addressed to him.

The teacher continued:

"My name is Emile Loubon." He wrote it on the board and then continued. "I am your class teacher and also your French teacher. Every Monday morning we will be in this classroom."

Then he spoke to us about the school rules and how the lessons were organized, gave us our schedule, and, after half an hour, asked us to fill in an information sheet that would help him get to know us better.

"First write down your surname and your first name, your address, your father's and mother's jobs, how many brothers and sisters you have . . ."

There was something charming about Monsieur

Loubon, with his square face, his wide jaw, his clearly defined mouth, his round brown eyes, and his matte complexion. His abundant brown hair was graying in places, aging him a little.

There were teachers with whom you felt sure straight away that everything was going to be all right. Monsieur Loubon was one of them. Then there were the others, like Madame Valard. Your first contact with her would put you off school. People like that raised doubts in your mind. You wondered why she had it in for you: because you were an Arab or because she didn't like the look of your face? But I had a nice face. I often looked at it in the mirror, and I thought it was amusing. You had to resign yourself to the fact that you couldn't please everybody.

While I was filling in my information sheet, the teacher walked around the classroom to collect the papers of those who had already finished. He reached my row of desks and bent his head over my shoulder to see my name. I turned around. And, at that moment, when our eyes met and came together, I felt that deep inside this man there was something that resembled me and that linked us together. I couldn't tell what it was. He went back to his desk, examined the forms and the corresponding faces closely, commented occasionally on a small detail, or asked for additional clarifications. Then he looked straight at me: my form was in his hands. I hated those situations where you had to talk about yourself. There it was; he was going to ask me some questions.

"How do you pronounce your name in Arabic?" he asked in a friendly tone.

Suddenly I felt empty inside. Fortunately the Tabouls were not in the class; otherwise what would I have replied? That I was not an Arab? Maybe there were other Tabouls around me? The teacher was waiting for an answer. How could I tell him that I didn't want to bare myself to all those pupils who were now watching me as if I was a circus animal? I felt like saying to him: "I am not who you think I am, my dear sir." But it was impossible. I had the feeling that he already knew everything about my story. So I replied:

"We say Azouz, M'sieur."

"Is it Algerian?!"

"Yes, M'sieur," I said sheepishly.

Now I was trapped. There was now no possible escape.

"Which region do you come from?"

"From Sétif, M'sieur. Well, I mean my parents come from there. I was born in Lyon, at Grange-Blanche hospital."

My immigrant neighbor from Paris was glued to my lips. He'd been listening carefully from the beginning. I felt like shouting to him: "Now you know everything. Are you happy? So stop looking at me like that."

"Did you used to live in Villeurbanne?"

"Yes."

"Where exactly?"

"The Avenue Monin, M'sieur."

"In the prefabs by the boulevard expressway?"

Puzzled by the teacher's intuition, terrified at the idea that he might know about Le Chaâba and the dirty conditions in which I used to live when I was small,

I replied that I indeed used to live in the prefabs. It sounded cleaner.

"And why did your parents move?"

"I don't know, M'sieur." In my head I was thinking: "This guy's pretty curious!"

Silence descended on the classroom for a few seconds. I told myself that now I could no longer hide my Moorish origins, that Yemma could now come and wait for me at the school gate. Then I realized that she would never come again. The damage had been done.

Monsieur Loubon started speaking again, this time to introduce himself:

"I too used to live in Algeria. In Tlemcen. It's near Oran. Do you know it?"

"No, M'sieur. I've never been to Algeria."

"So, let's see. I am French, but I was born in Algeria, and you were born in Lyon, but you're Algerian."

He smiled before continuing:

"I came to France some time after Independence."

"So you're a *pied-noir*, M'sieur?" I said to him, showing my knowledge.

"A repatriated citizen from Algeria, yes. One can also say pied-noir."

Then, nodding his head, he invited me to carry on with what I was saying.

"When my father used to live in Sétif, he worked for a boss who was also a pied-noir. He told me that. I even know his name: Barral."

"What did your father do in Sétif?"

"He was a journalist on Barral's farm."

"A journalist? On a farm?" the teacher asked, amazed.

"Yes, Sir. He looked after the sheep and the horses, he worked on the land, all day long."

He burst out laughing, then said:

"Oh! You mean he was hired as a journeyman?!"

"I don't know, Sir. My father always said he was a journalist. I'm just repeating what he said."

"No, no," said teacher. "The correct word is *journeyman*. You know, not all pieds-noirs owned a farm like Barral in Algeria."

I said nothing in response. All I knew was that my father said that the *binoirs* [pieds-noirs] didn't like the Arabs, especially those who worked with him in the factory. It seemed they were always saying to the Algerians on the building site: "You wanted your independence, and now you've come to work here!" They didn't understand. And neither did I. It seemed we should have returned home a long time ago.

The ten o'clock bell rang. The first French lesson had come to an end. Like the other pupils, I was putting away my books in my satchel and getting ready to leave the classroom when Monsieur Loubon asked me one last question, this time in Arabic—to be more precise, in Algerian Arabic, like we spoke at home. He asked me:

"Do you understand Arabic?"

In French, I answered him:

"Yes, I always speak Arabic with my parents."

"Right, good-bye for now. See you next Monday," he concluded, smiling.

My immigrant neighbor from the Eiffel Tower was looking at me like I was a god. Now his mouth was wide open.

"Did you know the teacher before?" he asked, burning with curiosity.

"No," I said. "It's the first time I've seen him."

"Holy shit!" He cracked off laughing. "You're so lucky!"

To put an end to this conversation, which was embarrassing me somewhat, I asked if he knew which classroom we now had to go to. He said he didn't know, then added:

"We can still sit together, if you want?"

"Yeah, yeah," I said. "That'll be really nice."

❨ ❨ ❨

"Azouz! Do you know how to say *Morocco* in Arabic?" Monsieur Loubon suddenly asked me as he was writing some sentence structures in the subjunctive on the blackboard.

The question did not surprise me. For several months now the teacher had been in the habit of having me speak in class about myself, my family, the Algeria that I didn't know and that I was discovering every day with him.

At home the Arabic we spoke would no doubt make the residents of Mecca flush with anger. For example, do you know how we would say *les allumettes* [matches]? *Li zalimite.* It was simple, and everybody understood it. And *automobile*? *La taumobile.* And *chiffon*? *Le chiffoun.* You see, it was a particular dialect that you could assimilate easily if your ear was sufficiently trained. *Mo-*

*rocco?* My parents had always said *el-Marroc*, putting a stress on the *o*. So I replied to Monsieur Loubon:

"For Morocco, Sir, we say *el-Marroc*!"

At first he seemed quite surprised; then he continued:

"Don't you say *el-Maghreb*?"

"Oh, no, Sir. My father and mother never use that word. To call someone a Moroccan, they say *Marrocci.*"

Clearly amused, Monsieur Loubon went on:

"In classical Arabic one says *el-Maghreb*, and it's written like this."

He drew some Arabic letters on the board, to the amazement of the pupils. As he was writing I said:

"I have heard my parents say that word."

He replied:

"Don't you know that, in Arabic, *Morocco* means 'the land of the setting sun'?"

"No, Sir."

Then he continued with the lesson for a few minutes before turning to me again:

"Do you know what this means?" he asked me again while drawing some hieroglyphics.

I said no. I didn't know how to read or write in Arabic.

"This is an *alif*, an *a*. This is an *l*, and this is another *a*," he explained. "So what does this word mean?"

I hesitated for a moment before replying.

"Ala!" I said, but without grasping the meaning of the word.

"Not 'Ala,'" said Monsieur Loubon. "'Allah'! Do you know who Allah is?"

I smiled a little at his Berber accent:

"Yes, Sir. Of course. Allah is the God of the Muslims."

"Well, that's how you write his name. You see, I speak Arabic nearly as well as you do."

He was really modest, my teacher. There he was, explaining my origins to me, demonstrating how little I knew of Arab culture, and he dared tell me that he spoke Arabic nearly as well as I did!

All around me the pupils were whispering. They were completely left out of it.

One evening, after school, Monsieur Loubon asked me to stay behind for a minute, so I waited until all the pupils had gone, a little embarrassed to be the subject of so much attention from the class teacher. He came up to me and handed me a book:

"Do you know this book by Jules Roy?"

I took the book and read the title: *Les Chevaux du soleil* [Horses in the sun].

"No, Sir, I don't know it." To be honest, I had never heard of Jules Roy. "But I do know Jules Renard!"

"Don't you know Jules Roy?"

"No, Sir."

"Then take this book straight away. It's a gift from me. Jules Roy is an Algerian like us, a really great Algerian writer."

"Is he dead, Sir?"

"Oh, no, not yet. He lives in France now."

I fidgeted with the book, turning it this way and that, waiting for Monsieur Loubon to put an end to this decidedly unusual conversation. He stared at the cover, with a dreamy look in his eyes. He must have been in his native Algeria at that moment. Then he resumed the conversation, without looking at me, with a touch of sadness in his voice:

"I was a teacher in Tlemcen. Oh, a wonderful town, Tlemcen! In my class I had only one Arab pupil. His name was Nasser. Nasser Bovabi. I remember him very well. It wasn't that long ago. He was a brilliant pupil. And you? What do want to do when you grow up?"

"I want to be president of the Republic of Algeria, Sir!" I said to him confidently.

"That's good. That's good. You must continue like that," he said, nodding his head. "Come on. It's getting late. Shall we leave?" he concluded after a few moments of silence.

"Yes, Sir."

We left the classroom and walked along the empty corridors of the lycée up to the main gate, where a few pupils were still standing around waiting for the school bus. They were all looking at us. Before we parted he said to me:

"You can keep *Les Chevaux du soleil*. It takes a long time to read. We'll talk about it another time. Good-bye."

I said good-bye, and I went down to the rue Terme. I was so delighted with the confidences shared by Monsieur Loubon that, when I returned home, I told my father that my pied-noir teacher had given me a book that talked about Algeria. He said:

"He's a good *broufissour* [teacher], he is!"

Then I told him that he could write Arabic and that

he had even written the name of Allah on the board, in front of the whole class. On hearing this my father, who adored Allah, went into raptures:

"*Allah Akbar!* [God is great!] The Almighty can win everyone's heart."

Then he added:

"Tomorrow you must ask him to come and eat a couscous here at home."

"No, Abboué," I answered. "You can't do that with teachers."

He seemed surprised, then replied:

"Why can't you do that? There's no harm in it. I'll buy him a *bouteille difaine* [bottle of wine]. The French like Algerian difaine, don't they?"

"Oh, no. I would be ashamed. Afterward all the pupils would make fun of me at school," I insisted vigorously.

Then Bouzid concluded naively:

"Here, take some money. Buy him a bottle, and take it to him."

I refused categorically. He did not make any other suggestions. There were lots of things like that that it was best not to get into much of a discussion about with Bouzid.

〈 〈 〈

"Sir! Sir! An inheritance is divided at the notary's. When you die, you make a will and say who you want to give your money to."

"That's good," Monsieur Loubon complimented a pupil.

Then, looking at another who had put his hand up:

"You don't agree?"

"Yes, Sir, but I wanted to say that, when the dead person hasn't left a will, then it's the law that divides everything between the heirs."

Monsieur Loubon gave another compliment. This morning he had started a debate on inheritance. I had not said anything yet because I did not understand anything of what the pupils were saying. Back home everything belonged to everybody. When someone died, those who were left behind did not share out the booty. It belonged to the family; that was all. In order not to be left out of the debate, I put my hand up:

"Sir, an inheritance cannot be divided. In the family it is the eldest brother who is responsible for everything when somebody dies."

Protests rang out in the class. Some pupils burst out laughing. I continued in a louder voice:

"You can laugh. But at home that's what happens. My father has a little house with a garden—well, it belongs to all of us, his children. We'll never divide things like that!"

At the back of the class a nasty voice rang out:

"Only savages behave like that!"

This provoked general mirth. Other pupils put up their hands very high to contribute to the discussion. Monsieur Loubon stood utterly still and silent. He stared at the pupil who had spoke about savages. A heavy silence descended on the class, and the pupils put their hands down. The teacher looked cross. Then, after a moment, he said calmly:

"You're going to apologize to your classmate."

The whole class turned toward the miscreant. He hung down his head, staring at his shoes, and muttered a muffled "Sorry." He was no doubt as surprised as I was by Monsieur Loubon's reaction.

"Now take a double sheet of exercise paper, all of you. You're going to write for the rest of the lesson," the teacher said emphatically, without any further explanation.

The discussion was over. To a considerable extent because of me. During the dictation I did not dare look at anyone. What must they think of me now? That I was a creep. In the Ecole Léo-Lagrange the Arabs in the class said I wasn't one of them because I wasn't at the bottom of the class with them. Here it wouldn't be long before the French pupils started telling tales about me because Monsieur Loubon and I had Algeria in common. But I wasn't afraid of them. I was a little embarrassed, that was all.

❬ ❬ ❬

An earlier humiliation, etched in my mind, came back to me. When Madame Valard returned the essays we had done a week earlier as homework, she stopped in front of me, stared at me, and, with an ugly grin at the corner of her lips, spat out:

"You're just a fraud. You have copied Maupassant very badly."

At first I blushed, dismayed by the accusation; then I tried to defend myself while pupils roared with laughter all around me.

"M'dame, I didn't copy Maupassant. I didn't know

he had written that story. It was the teacher at my old school who told me the story," I replied naively.

She, however, only too happy to have recognized Guy de Maupassant, even in so-called plagiarized form, shamed me in front of the whole class, shouting:

"And to top it all you're lying! I had given you one out of twenty for putting ink to paper, but now I'll give you zero. That's what you deserve."

Yet, it was Monsieur Grand who had told us about the misadventure that had befallen a poor old man in a village, decades earlier. The poor guy had a habit of collecting all the odds and ends that he found lying around, in the hope that one day he would be able to make use of them. One morning, right in the middle of the main village square, he had bent down to pick up a piece of string from the ground, perhaps to use it as a shoestring. He had slipped it furtively into his pocket, but at that very moment the butcher, sitting in front of his shop, had been watching him closely. The next day a serious piece of news shook the village: the local clergyman, returning from the neighboring town, had lost his wallet, probably, it was thought, in the main square. The butcher thought he had seen and understood everything. Because of the piece of string the old man was taken off to prison.

The same misfortune that had befallen the old man had struck me at the hand of Madame Valard. I had not stolen anything from Monsieur Maupassant, but I had been condemned on suspicion. From that day on all the pupils, except for Babar, thought I was crafty, if not plain dishonest, and every time we had to write an essay at home I did everything I could to avoid falling into the trap of originality. I would write a couple of pages about the sea, the mountains, the swirling autumn leaves, or the snowy winter coat, but Madame Valard still didn't like my work. Now she would write in the margin in red: "Uninteresting! Lacks originality! Too vague!"

At the Lycée Saint-Exupéry I was Monsieur Loubon's pet, but my essay marks were often barely adequate. The French pupils wrote better than me. Monsieur Loubon was a little disappointed. He must have thought I was incapable of having any original ideas because my parents were illiterate. I felt somewhat bitter.

The older students in all the lycées and the bus drivers had been on strike for several weeks now. At Saint-Ex, our lessons were completely disrupted, and the summer holidays looked like they were going to be long. One Monday morning I walked to school to find out what was happening to our classes. I felt some pangs of remorse vis-à-vis Monsieur Loubon, but the fact was that many pupils hadn't been to lessons for quite a long time. That morning, not having prepared any specific program, he suggested a free choice of topics for composition at home and sent us off into the street. Allah had guided my footsteps for I had been waiting for this opportunity for several long months and now a pied-noir was offering it to me on a plate. Racism. That was what I knew I had to write about in my essay.

( ( (

I spent several days writing the story. Once upon a time there was an Arab boy. He and his family had just arrived in Lyon. The child had not yet made a single friend in the neighborhood, and, on the first day at school, he found himself all alone among dozens of boys and girls who all knew each other, who were laughing and joking together. When the bell rang, the boy watched the children go into the playground and, after hesitating for a moment, decided to return home to his mother.

I asked Zohra to read my work. She corrected the grammatical mistakes and gently made fun of me because the writing sounded like a desperate cry for help and I had exaggerated a little.

The last days of June marched on fast. All the buses were still paralyzed by strikes, so I preferred taking bicycle rides with the kids from the rue de la Vieille rather than wasting my time going to school. However, one Tuesday my father sent me to school to get a school attendance certificate. Outside the entrance, in the middle of a group of pupils who were chatting quietly, I recognized my immigrant Parisian friend. As soon as he saw me he ran up to me, his face lit up, and then, offering me his hand in greeting, he said:

"Weren't you here yesterday?"

"No. Why? Were there lots of pupils here?"

I was scared for a minute in case I had been the only one absent, but he reassured me:

"No. There were only nine of us. But the class teacher returned the essays."

His face became more and more mysterious, and his lips widened into a smile.

"So what?"

"Well, you got seventeen out of twenty. The best

grade in the class. The teacher even read us your composition. He said he would keep it as an example of good work."

I put my bike down on the ground and asked for more details. My body was paralyzed by emotion. I felt like climbing up trees, doing dangerous somersaults, breaking my bicycle as a sacrifice.

"What else did he say?"

"Nothing else. He was sorry that you weren't there."

"And where is he now?"

I took a few steps toward the playground.

"He's not there. There's no one in the school. I think school's finished now."

In the name of Allah! Allah Akbar! I felt proud of my fingers. At last I was intelligent. I, Azouz Begag, the only Arab in the class, had got the best grade in the class, ahead of all the French pupils! I was dizzy with pride. I could tell my father that I was better that all the French pupils in the class. He would jump with joy.

But why had the teacher read my homework out to everybody? It was only for him that I had written it. I thought briefly about all those who would have certainly not missed the opportunity to put us both in the same basket as dune coons. It didn't matter. I felt as strong as an ox.

That evening, when I got back home, I told my father that the pied-noir teacher had given me the best grade in the class, better than all the French pupils. He said to me:

"Tell him that I'd like to invite him to come and eat a couscous. With wine, if he wants."

"No, Abboué," I replied firmly again.

"Then take some money. Go and buy him a bottle of wine," he insisted again.

I said:

"No, Abboué. In any case school's finished."

A strange glimmer flashed in his eyes; then he said in his most mystical voice:

"Come. Come here!"

I went toward him.

"Ouaiche, Abboué?"

"Come closer; I want to tell you something."

I went up to him.

"Sit down."

I did as he told me. He then started speaking in a soft voice as if he was about to confide some secret prophecies to me:

"You see, my son . . ."

"No, Abboué."

"Let me speak," he said. "I'm going to tell you something important."

"Go on, Abboué."

"You see, my son, God is above everything. For each and every one of us, Allah guides our *mektoub* [destiny] — mine, yours, your binoir broufissour's."

I smiled slightly.

"You mustn't laugh at that, my son."

"I'm not laughing, Abboué!"

"Do you think it's an accident that you, an Arab, did better than all the French pupils in the school? And your broufissour! Who taught him to write *Allah* in our language?"

"He learned it by himself, Abboué!"

At that point Bouzid put on his most serious look and concluded:

"No, my son. Allah. It is Allah who guides us. Nobody else."

Then he suggested:

"You should go to the koranic school on Saturday mornings."

On hearing that, I rebelled:

"Oh, no, Abboué, I have enough work at school as it is."

"All right, all right. As you like, my son. You decide."

Then Yemma called us to dinner in the kitchen. I took my plate in my hands, and I went toward the sofa.

"Where are you going?" asked Bouzid.

"I'm going to eat while watching television," I replied, sure of myself.

Bouzid tried to protest, but I cut him short straight away by saying:

"It's Allah who's guiding my hand."

Looking at Yemma, my father said:

"He's a real devil, that child!"

Then he burst out laughing.

⟪ ⟪ ⟪

A few days later I received my school report in the mailbox. Monsieur Loubon was very pleased with my work. An additional little note explained that an information meeting was to be held for parents and teachers on the following Saturday. This time Bouzid, Yemma, and Zohra went. My sister's role was that of a translator. In spite of my entreaties my father took two bottles of Sidi-Brahim wine in a bag to thank the teacher who could write *Allah* in Arabic.

I didn't want to be present at the meeting. I stayed at home, watching television, and waited for them. And, as soon as they returned, Zohra, full of admiration, spoke first:

"As soon as we entered the classroom he asked, 'Are you Azouz's family?' and then he left everyone else to come and talk to us."

I smiled. Bouzid carried on:

"He asked why you hadn't come. And then he was very pleased with the bottles of Sidi-Brahim."

"I think he was a little embarrassed," said Yemma, before explaining: "The other parents were giving us nasty looks."

I felt all the more happy.

〘 〘 〘

After Monsieur Loubon's praise and confirmation of my admission to the second year at the Lycée Saint-Ex-upéry, I was treated like a full-blown scholar at home.

School was finished. The holidays came, and I had fun. I could watch television to my heart's content; Bouzid gave in to my wishes.

My father was tired. I was the only one who could make him laugh from time to time—when I disobeyed his orders. At each opportunity I never failed to remind him of what he always said to us:

"You work at school while I work at the factory."

So, having been congratulated on my schoolwork, I granted myself almost total freedom at home. Caught in his own trap, Bouzid could only smile and give in. He was proud. His children would not become laborers like him. One day they would wear a doctor's or an engineer's white overall and return to Sétif. They would be rich. They would build a house. And too bad if every day he had to work ten hours to pay the rent, the electricity, and the water.

Sometimes it seemed to me that he was getting used to his new life, that he was thinking less and less of Le Chaâba. But the next day he would swear at Yemma, curse her for having wanted to move, and escape for three or four days to his old house, leaving us without a cent.

Bouzid had become unpredictable.

( ( (

That afternoon, just after the children's program on TV, I took a nap. I had been trying to read *Les Chevaux du soleil* by Jules Roy, but before the end of the second page I succumbed to the enervating July heat.

"It's three o'clock," Yemma called to me. "What's wrong with you? Are you ill?"

Through the haze I told her my state of heath was perfect.

"Why are you always indoors like this?" she said to me. "You should go and play outside with your friends."

At that moment there was a knock on the door. Whenever someone came to the door, Yemma became anxious, as if she was always expecting bad news. So she murmured between her teeth:

"Please let it be good fortune! Good fortune! Go away evil; get away from us!"

Before she went to open the door, she examined the flat, adjusted a curtain, picked up a towel, and tidied a pair of shoes. She asked, first in French, then in Arabic:

"*Qui ci? Chkoun?* [Who is it?]"

Then, turning to me:

"It's your friends; they've come to fetch you."

"Let them in, Yemma!"

Ali Saadi kissed my mother. Kamel did the same. Babar shook her hand.

"We're going to the rue de la Vieille," said Ali. "Are you doing anything?"

I said I wasn't.

Mother gave us each a piece of semolina galette, and we left. As we went downstairs I asked Kamel:

"Where are we going?"

Ali replied in a fired-up voice:

"We've got a date with some women in the Place Sathonay. There are four of them."

Kamel rubbed his hands, crinkled his Chinese-looking eyes a little more, opened his mouth, dotted with yellow teeth, and laughed excitedly:

"We're going to feel 'em up."

Ali added:

"This time I am going for the tall one; I'm going to get it on with her in a traboule. Last time I touched her all over; she didn't mind."

Babar, a little more reserved than his buddies, whose egos were inflated with *harissa* [hot spice] and Tunisian peppers, didn't say a word but was amused at their expressions.

Ali continued:

"Kamel will do best with the ugly one. You and Babar, you can take the other two."

The sex maniac countered:

"I don't care if she's fat. I'm still gonna feel her up."

With saliva dripping from his tongue, he got more and more excited on the stairs.

I had all kinds of thoughts racing in my head. I wanted to get to the square quickly, just like Babar, but I didn't let it show.

Martine, Ali's date, was sitting alone at the foot of the statue of Sergeant Blandan. We walked up to her.

"Where are your friends?"

"They went to the swimming pool. I'm on my own," the cutie replied.

Kamel went pale. Babar smiled. Neither of them said anything. In my head the castle I had been building in the air tumbled down. Embarrassed by this delicate situation, Ali said to Martine:

"Right, well, let's go for a little walk. You coming?"

The divine, beautifully sun-tanned creature got up, signaling her consent, gratified us with an out-of-this-world smile, and took Ali's hand.

"See you later!" shouted the lucky guy.

The couple plunged into the nearby alleyways, heading for the traboules. Kamel was having difficulty keeping calm. He was cursing every woman on earth with the exception of our mothers and sisters. We hung around in the Place Sathonay for two hours, waiting for

Ali to come back. We eyed all the girls as they crossed the square, lifted up about a dozen skirts, and looked at the color of their undies. Kamel ran crazily after all the females, his right hand stretched out before him, like someone trying to catch a hen in a farmyard. Every time he touched a target he turned toward Babar and me and called out like an animal:

"Look! Look!"

Then he laughed. And we laughed. I would have liked to touch the girls too. But I was ashamed. Kamel wasn't afraid of getting slapped on the face or being told: "Dirty Arab, go back to where you came from." He was laughing. And, when a girl objected, he would say to her, "Do you want it? Do you want it?" then stick his hand between her legs.

Ali finally came back, alone. Martine had preferred to take a different way home.

"Well, did you score?" said Kamel.

By way of an answer Ali gave a smile that said everything. Then, after thinking for a moment, he added:

"Do you know where a woman's pussy is? It's not there, like us; it's between her legs," he said, showing the way with his finger.

Everybody was amazed.

"Are you sure?" asked Kamel. "I've seen girls, and, well, their thing was out front, not between the legs, but I guess they were little."

Babar pieced it all together:

"Yeah, when they grow up, their thing must shift from here to there."

He showed us with his finger.

"Shut it! Shut it!" Ali interrupted. "Her three friends are coming."

Back from the swimming pool, they greeted us with a slightly mocking air that made me lose my cool. Only Ali, sure of himself as ever, was able to keep the conversation going while trying to prepare a new plan. Kamel's ardor dampened. We sat on a bench to chat. Suddenly Babar turned toward me and whispered:

"Your father! Over there. Look. He's coming this way."

At these words I was shaken by a violent conflagration. I saw my father, looking very agitated, coming toward me from the rue Sergent-Blandan. I could not think for a few seconds. If he were to see me with girls, I would never dare look him in the eyes again. I quickly excused myself from the present company, claiming to have some urgent business so as not to lose face in front of the girls. Bent double as low as possible, I took to my heels in the direction of the rue de la Vieille. Bouzid must have seen me. Then I wasn't sure. I didn't have long to wait for the answer. I had hardly gone a few yards when a terrible voice rang through the Place Sathonay. The pigeons flew off with much flapping of wings.

"Razzouz!" shouted the old man.

I pretended not to hear. He warned me:

"Razzouz! I saw you."

In the square passersby turned to look at him, then at me. No more girls for me now! I went up to him, trapped like a rabbit. In Arabic, he screamed:

"Why did you run away when I called you?"

"I wasn't running away. I was going to buy a bottle of lemonade in the store."

"Are you making fun of me?"

I did not answer for fear of making things worse.

He continued:

"Where's your brother?"

"I don't know."

"Right, you go back home. I'm going to look for that hallouf."

"Why, Abboué?"

"Go back home," he said. "It's none of your business."

Then he went wandering around the neighborhood. Something serious must have happened for him to get into such a state. I was suddenly scared. I ran home. Zohra opened the door for me. She did not look happy and said:

"Have you seen Dad?"

I said yes. She went on:

"And Staf? Where is he?"

"I don't know. Dad has already asked me that."

In the kitchen Yemma was crying, her face full of despair.

"What's the matter, Yemma?" I said to her.

She carried on crying, her hands over her eyes, without opening her mouth. I turned to Zohra:

"What's happened?"

"We've received a recorded letter from the administrators who let the apartment to us."

"So?"

"We have to move," she said dejectedly.

My throat tightened. Suddenly, in my head, everything came crashing down. It was like an earthquake, swallowing up Babar, Ali, and Kamel, the rue de la Vieille, Le Chaâba, the Lycée Saint-Exupéry, and Monsieur Loubon. Everything went blurred in my mind. My head ached. My knees felt weak.

"Where's the letter, Zohra?"

"Over there, on the table. Don't touch it; otherwise he's going to get even more worked up."

Bouzid returned a few minutes later, yelling like a madman. He went into the kitchen, hesitated for a moment, then went straight to the letter, took it in his hands, looked at it for a while, and cursed the son he had been unable to find.

"The dog! Never here when he's needed. This time I'll show him what's what."

Then he turned to me and shouted:

"Come here, you! Come and read this again for me. Explain to me what they're saying in it."

"Abboué, he's not going to add any more to what I said," said Zohra.

The old man became frantic:

"I told you not to speak any more. I'm going to find you a husband so you won't bother me any more."

My sister slipped out, shocked at having aroused so much paternal love.

I read the letter. It said that the apartment we lived in was going to have a new owner, who intended to sell it. They therefore proposed that we buy the apartment or find somewhere else to live. I translated into Arabic. Bouzid's eyes were wide open. It wasn't difficult to see the turmoil going on inside his head. He turned toward my mother. She was still crying. She was crying because of him but also because of the letter. Suddenly he opened his mouth as if he was going to spit out his tobacco and started screaming:

"It serves you right! It serves you right. You wanted to leave Le Chaâba, and here's the result of it. Where are we going to go now? To hell with you! You all deserve to go to hell. All of you."

Then he took up the letter in his hand again.

"I'll go off on my own," he went on. "That'll teach you a lesson."

Then, thinking about the property manager:

"But what about these thieves?! For a start, they have no right to throw me out of here. I pay the rent, litriziti, *la sarge* [the communal charges]. I pay for everything. Why do they want to throw me out? I'll go and see them tomorrow."

( ( (

He did go to see the manager, after work; then he came home, resigned. Like a wounded animal he said to Staf:

"You're going to read the paper every day to see if there are any apartments to rent in the neighborhood."

"Did you go to see the manager on your own?" asked Staf, naively.

"And do you think I need you to speak to French people for me? How do you think I managed before I brought you over from El-Ouricia? Do you think I couldn't speak? It wasn't you who found me a job, was it?"

"What did the manager say?" Staf went on.

The old man calmed down.

"He wanted to give us an apartment straight away in the *zip* [housing project]. I said no. I won't go anywhere too far from work."

"So how long can we stay here for?" asked Zohra.

"They told me they were going to look into some other *loug'mas* [accommodations]. We'll have to wait."

I ventured:

"And if we don't want to leave here, what will they do to us?"

"*Ils nous xspilsent dehors.* [They'll throw us out.] They'll throw all our stuff out. *Le rigissoure* [property manager] has told me."

The manager must have brandished the threat of expulsion at my father for him to be suddenly so well tempered with us. He must have been terrified. Ready to accept the first solution that presented itself. Le Chaâba perhaps . . .

( ( (

The very next day the manager knocked on our door. In spite of the misfortune he was bringing on us, Bouzid invited him into our home, offered him coffee, spoke to him about all sorts of things, thinking the man was going to announce some happy piece of news. Unruffled, the manager finished his coffee and said what he had to say:

"Monsieur Begag, you know you've gone past the date set. Now we've found you an apartment in the La Duchère housing project. It's a three-bedroom apartment, bigger than this one, with more light, and not too far from here either. Hardly fifteen minutes away. So? What is your decision?"

Bouzid had leaned both forearms on the table. He looked like he was thinking, but I knew already that he was going to accept. He could not reject this ultimate proposal. The manager insisted:

"It's the last offer I can make you. After that your furniture will be thrown out into the street. You've been warned. Expulsion. You know what that means, don't you?"

My father slumped in his chair:

He asked: "*A la Dichire, y en a li magasas, l'icoule bour li zafas?* [Are there shops and a school for the children in La Duchère?]"

"There's everything you want there," the manager said firmly.

"*J'y va y aller bour la fisite.* [I'll go and take a visit.]"

"Whenever you want to," said the manager, satisfied.

He got up from his chair smiling, held out his hand to my father, then blurted out:

"Fortunately you are an intelligent man; otherwise this business would have ended badly."

Bouzid got up in his turn, his eyes drawn, staring and fearful. As he held out his hand he attempted to put on a polite smile and said:

"Thank you."

"You're welcome," replied the man. "So when are you going back to your country?"

"*Hou là là* [Goodness me]!" said my father, raising his arms to the sky. "*Ci Allah qui dicide ça. Bi titre, j'va bartir l'anni brouchaine, bi titre li mois brouchain.* [That's for Allah to decide. Maybe I'll go back next year, maybe next month.]"

# Glossaries and Guide to Nonstandard Pronunciation of French

These appendices are based on those included in the original French edition of *Le Gone du Chaâba*. In consultation with the author, they have been expanded and adapted to meet the needs of English-speaking readers.

## Bouzidien Pronunciation of French

There are significant differences between French and Arabic where vowels and consonants are concerned. For example, there is no letter P or V in Arabic. Where those letters occur in French words used by Arabic-speakers such as Bouzid, they are pronounced as *b* and *f*. Neither does Arabic have sounds such as the French *on*, *in*, *an*, or *u*. Once you know this, you can understand the Bouzidien pronunciation of French.

EXAMPLES OF WORDS AND PHRASES (in order of appearance in the text) *Bouzidien pronunciation followed by standard French pronunciation followed by English translation*

*l'bomba*   la pompe; hand pump.
*la saboune d'Marsaille*   le savon de Marseille; Marseilles soap.

*le baissaine*   le baissaine; pool holding pumped water.

*binouar*   peignoir; dressing gown.

*eau de colonne*   eau de Cologne; eau de Cologne.

*moufissa*   mauvais sang; worries.

*finiane*   fainéant; lazy bum.

*bouariane*   bon à rien; good-for-nothing.

*la bitaine*   la putain; hooker.

*la boulicia*   la police; police.

*le koussaria*   le commissariat; police station.

*li zbour*   le sport; sport.

*l'ballou*   le ballon; soccer ball.

*l'bidoufile*   le bidonville; shantytown.

*A l'angar Birache*   A la gare Perrache; To the Perrache train
   station.

*li zou*   les œufs; eggs.

*ria di to!*   rien du tout; nothing at all.

*quinquis*   quinquet; oil lamp.

*litriziti*   l'éléctricité; electricity.

*Bijou*   Peugeot; Peugeot (automobile).

*souffage satral*   chauffage central; central heating.

*Zalouprix d'hallouf*   Saloperie d'hallouf; You dirty pig.

***Zaloupard di Grand Bazar! Zalouprix di Mounouprix!*** Sa-
   lopard du Grand Bazar! Saloperie de Monoprix! You dirty
   pig! You filthy swine!

*espèce de fainiaine*   espèce de fainéant; good-for-nothing.

*Digage dlà*   Dégage de là; Get out of there.

*la bart'mâ*   l'appartement; apartment.

*blouc*   le bloc; kitchen countertop.

*tababrisi*   tabac à priser; chewing tobacco.

*l'icoule*   l'école; school.

*kouci kouça*   comme ci, comme ça; so so.

*l'alcoufe*   l'alcôve; alcove.

*la tilifiziou*   la télévision; television.

*Grache-Blache*   Grange-Blanche; Grange-Blanche (hospital
   name).

*binoirs*   pieds-noirs; white settlers in North Africa.

*li zalimite*   les allumettes; matches.

*la taumobile*   l'automobile; automobile.

*le chiffoun*   le chiffon; duster.

*El-Marroc*   Le Maroc; Morocco.

*broufissour*   professeur; teacher.

*bouteille difaine*   bouteille de vin; bottle of wine.

*Qui ci?*   Qui est-ce?; Who is it?

*la sarge*   les charges; communal charges in a condominium.

*ZIP*   ZUP (Zone à Urbaniser en Priorité); housing project.

*loug'mas*   logements; accommodations.

*le rigissoure*   le régisseur; property-manager.

Beware of *faux amis* (false friends) such as "le filou" ("crook" in standard French; "vélo" [bicycle] in Bouzidien)

EXAMPLES OF COMPLETE SENTENCES *Bouzidien pronunciation followed by Standard French pronunciation followed by English translation*

*Tan a rizou, Louisa, li bitaines zi ba bou bour li zafas!*
Tu as raison, Louise, les putains c'est pas bon pour les enfants!
You're right, Louise. Hookers are no good for children!

*Oui, missiou! Trois falises y dou cartoux. Si tau!*
Oui, Monsieur. Trois valises et deux cartons. C'est tout!
Yes, Monsieur. Three suitcases and two boxes. That's all.

*Ti vous dinagi? J'vais ti douni di dinagima!*
Tu veux déménager? Je vais te donner du déménagement!
Ya wanna move? I'll give y'a move!

*Atre! Atre boire café. T'en as pas peur?*
Entre! Entre boire un café. Tu n'en as pas peur?
Come in! Come in and have a coffee. You're not afraid?

*Fout'-moi l'camp da l'alcoufe!*
Fout'-moi le camp de l'alcove.
Get the hell out of the alcove.

*Une briouche avec li chicoulat.*
Une brioche avec du chocolat.
A chocolate bun.

*Ils nous xspilsent dehors.*
Ils nous expulsent dehors.
They'll throw us out.

*A la Dichire, y en a li magasas, l'icoule bour li zafas?*
A la Duchère, y a-t-il des magasins, l'école pour les enfants?
Are there shops and a school for the children at la Duchère?

*J'y va y aller bour la fisite.*
Je vais y aller pour la visite.
I'll go and take a visit.

*Ci Allah qui dicide ça. Bi titre, j'va bartir l'anni brouchaine,*
*bi titre li mois brouchain.*
C'est Allah qui decide ça. Peut-être que je vais y partir
l'année prochaine, peut-être le mois prochain.
That's for Allah to decide. Maybe I'll go back next year,
maybe next month.

**Bouzidien Words** (Arabic dialect spoken by natives of Sétif)
*Bouzidien followed by standard French followed by English trans-*
*lation or explanation*

*Abboué*   Papa; Dad.
*Aïd*   fête musulmane célébrant la fin du Ramadan et à
l'occasion de laquelle des millions de moutons de toutes
les nationalités laissent leur peau; Muslim festivals (Aïd
Esseghir and Aïd El Kebir) celebrating the end of Rama-

dan and the Sacrifice of Abraham, the latter marked by the slaughtering of sheep.

*Allah Akbar*   Dieu est grand; God is great.

*Artaille*   Très gros mot!; Very strong swear word!

*bendir*   sorte de tambour oriental; drums.

*binouar*   peignoir *or* robe algérienne; A corruption of the French word "peignoir" (dressing gown), used by women in Le Chaâba to refer to a traditional Algerian dress.

*bitelma*   toilettes, sanitaires; toilet, privy.

*Chaâba*   Terrain vague avec des lieux d'habitation mal faits; patch of spare land containing roughly improvised dwellings.

*chemma*   tabac à priser; chewing tobacco.

*Chkoun*   Qui est-ce? Who is it?

*chorba*   soupe populaire algérienne; Algerian soup made with tomatoes, coriander and lamb.

*chritte*   gant de crin; loofah.

*djnoun* (plural djen)   démons, mauvais esprits; demons, evil spirits.

*gandoura*   gandoura; robe.

*Gaouri, Gaouria*   Français, Française; Frenchman, Frenchwoman.

*Gharbi*   Bienvenue (pour une femme); Welcome (addressed to a woman).

*gourbi*   habitat délabré; hovel.

*guittoun*   tente; tent.

*hachema*   honte; shame.

*hallouf*   cochon; Arabic term meaning "pork," the consumption of which is prohibited to Muslims; by extension, unclean or distrusted people or objects.

*harissa*   harissa; harissa (hot spice).

*henna*   henné; henna.

*kaissa*   gant de toilette; wash cloth.

*Labaisse?*   Ça va?; You okay?

*marabout*   marabout; marabout (holy man).

*Mektoub*   Destin, ce qui est écrit; Destiny, that which is
written.

*mrabta*   Femme marabout; female marabout (holy person).

*Ouaiche?*   Quoi?; What is it?

*Ouallah*   Au nom d'Allah; In the name of Allah.

*oued*   rivière; river.

*rhaïn*   oeil, mauvais oeil, scoumone; eye, evil eye, bad
luck.

*Roumi*   Français; French person.

*Salam oua rlikoum*   Bonjour; Good-day.

*tahar*   circonciseur de zénanas; circumciser.

*Yemma*   Maman; Mom.

*zénana*   quiquette; wiener.


*Azouzien Words* (Slang spoken by natives of Lyon)
*Azouzien followed by English translation or explanation*

*Baraque*   shack; basic unit in a shantytown, key form of
housing for Algerian immigrants in the 1960s.

*Bôche*   stone, pebble.

*Braque*   bicycle.

*Gone*   kid.

*Pâti*   garbage collector or tramp.

*Radée de pierres*   hail of stones.

*Traboule*   alleyway running through a block of houses,
typical of the Croix-Rousse neighborhood.

*Vogue*   Fair in Lyon.


*Other French Terms* *French followed by English explanation*

*école*   see *lycée.*

*galette*   flat cake; as used by Algerians such as members of

Begag's family, denotes home-made bread made out of semolina.

*lycée*    French high school. Until the 1960s, most French children did not continue their formal education beyond elementary school (*école primaire*, commonly shortened to *école*). Admission to the *lycée* at the age of 11 or 12 was reserved for only a minority of children and was therefore highly prized. With the raising of the school leaving age to 16, a middle school (*collège*) attended by all pupils from the age of 11 onwards was introduced between elementary school and the *lycée*. Today, entry to the *lycée* typically takes place at the age of 15. As the young Begag passed through the school system before the general introduction of the *collège* (middle school), he moved straight from *école* to *lycée*.

*Vercingétorix*    A Gaulish chief of the Roman period, generally regarded as one of the earliest ancestors of the modern French nation. A nineteenth century history textbook widely used in French and colonial schools contained a now legendary reference to "Nos ancêtres les Gaullois (our ancestors the Gauls)…" which has remained emblematic of the role of education in fostering a sense of nationhood among the French. The use of this textbook in colonies such as Algeria also typified the insensitivity of the French authorities towards the cultural heritage of non-Europeans.

# Books and Articles about Azouz Begag and "Beur" Literature

Aitsiselmi, Farid. "La Langue des Beurs: De Charef à Begag." *Interface*, no. 5 (spring 2000): 27–38.

Armbrecht, Thomas J. D. "Beur Writing as a Self-Definition: Azouz Begag's *Béni ou le paradis privé* and Leïla Sebbar's *Leïla, 17 ans, brune . . . .*" In *Cultures transnationales en France: Des "Beurs" aux . . . ?* ed. Hafid Gafaïti, 163–81. Paris: L'Harmattan, 2001.

"Azouz Begag de A à Z." Special issue of *Expressions maghrébines*, vol. 1, no. 2 (winter 2002).

Bernard, Philippe. "Zouzou retrouve Georgette." In *La Crème des Beurs: De l'immigration à l'intégration*, 47–64. Paris: Seuil, 2004.

Bonn, Charles, ed. *Littératures des immigrations*. 2 vols. Paris: L'Harmattan, 1995.

———, ed. *Migrations des identités et des textes entre l'Algérie et la France, dans les littératures des deux rives*. Paris: L'Harmattan, 2004.

"Cities/Banlieues." Special issue of *Contemporary French and Francophone Studies*, vol. 8, nos. 1 and 2 (January and April 2004).

Desplanques, François. "Begag et Tadjer, entre sourire et gouaille."

*Itinéraires et contacts de cultures*, no. 14 (July 1991): 177– 82.

Durmelat, Sylvie. "Petite Histoire du mot 'beur.'" *French Cultural Studies* 9, no. 2 (June 1998): 191–207.

Emery, Meghan. "Azouz Begag's *Le Gone du Chaâba*: Discovering the Beur Subject in the Margins." *French Review* 77, no. 6 (May 2004): 1151–64.

Gafaïti, Hafid, ed. *Cultures transnationales en France: Des "Beurs" aux . . . ?* Paris: L'Harmattan, 2001.

Hänsch, Verena. "Schreiben in Zwischenräumen: Azouz Begag." In *Die Kinder der Immigration/Les Enfants de l'immigration*, ed. Ernstpeter Ruhe, 205–9. Würzburg: Königshausen & Neumann, 1999.

Hargreaves, Alec G. *Voices from the North African Immigrant Community in France: Immigration and Identity in Beur Fiction*. Oxford: Berg, 1991. 2nd, expanded ed., Oxford: Berg, 1997.

———. *La Littérature beur: Un guide bio-bibliographique*. New Orleans: CELFAN Edition Monographs, 1992.

———, ed. *Minorités postcoloniales anglophones et francophones: Etudes culturelles comparées*. Paris: L'Harmattan, 2004.

Hargreaves, Alec G., and Mark McKinney, eds. *Post-Colonial Cultures in France*. London: Routledge, 1997.

Ireland, Susan, and Patrice J. Proulx, eds. *Immigrant Narratives in Contemporary France*. Westport CT: Greenwood, 2001.

Keil, Regina. "Entre le politique et l'esthétique: Littérature 'beur' ou littérature 'franco-maghrébine'?" *Itinéraires et contacts de cultures* 14 (July 1991): 159–69.

———. "Des hommes et des arbres: La déterritorialisation du discours identitaire maghrébin: Lecture croisée de Mohammed Dib (*L'Enfant maure*) et Azouz Begag (*L'Ilet-aux-Vents*)." In *Exils croisés*, vol. 2 of *Littératures des immigrations*, ed. Charles Bonn, 19–33. Paris: L'Harmattan, 1995.

Landrin, Sophie. "Azouz Begag, notable lyonnais." *Le Monde*, May 11, 2005.

Laronde, Michel. *Autour du roman beur: Immigration et identité.* Paris: L'Harmattan, 1993.

Laronde, Michel, ed. *L'Ecriture décentrée: La langue de l'Autre dans le roman contemporain.* Paris: L'Harmattan, 1996.

Lay-Chenchabi, Kathryn. "Writing for Their Lives: Three Beur Writers Discover Themselves." *Mots pluriels,* no. 17 (April 2001). Available at http://www.arts.uwa.edu.au/MotsPluriels/ MP1701klc.html.

Magnan, Sally Sieloff. "Young *Beur* Heroes: Helping Students Understand Tensions of Multicultural France." *French Review* 77, no. 5 (April 2004): 914–29.

Mainil, Jean. "Le Baiser de la femme speakerine: Télévision et romans beurs." *Sites* 1, no. 1 (spring 1997): 125–40.

McConnel, Daphne. "Questions of Cultural and National Identity in Two Novels by Second-Generation Maghrebians in France." *LittéRéalité* 12, no. 1 (2000): 39–50.

Mdarhri-Alaoui, Abdallah. "Analyse comparative et didactique des incipit du *Passé simple* de Driss Chraïbi et de *Béni ou le Paradis privé* d'Azouz Begag." *Itinéraires et contacts de culture,* no. 26 (July 1998): 89–103.

Mebarki, Belkacem, "Azouz Begag, ou les coups de gueule identitaires d'un Beur." *Insaniyat,* no. 10 (January–April 2001): 67–72.

Mehrez, Samia. "Azouz Begag: Un di Zafas di Bidoufile (Azouz Begag: Un des enfants du bidonville): On the Beur Writer: A Question of Territory." *Yale French Studies,* no. 82 (1993): 25–42.

———. "*Ahmed de Bourgogne*: The Impossible Autobiography of a Clandestine." *Alif,* no. 22 (2002): 36–71.

Naudin, Marie. "Formation post-moderne des Beurs chez Mehdi Charef, Leïla Sebbar et Azouz Begag." *Francographies,* no. 4 (1995): 97–103.

O'Riley, Michael. "Of Earthquakes and Cultural Sedimentation: The Origins of Postcolonial Shock Waves in Azouz Begag's

Zenzela." *Francophone Post-Colonial Cultures: Critical Essays,* ed. Salhi Kamal, 296–307. Lanham MD: Lexington, 2003.

Ruhe, Ernstpeter, ed. *Die Kinder der Immigration/Les Enfants de l'immigration.* Würzburg: Königshausen & Neumann, 1999.

Sessa, Jacqueline. "Le 'Beur' dans les romans de Mehdi Charef et d'Azouz Begag." *New Comparison,* no. 10 (autumn 1990): 60–71.

Sourdot, Marc. "Un Héros recentré: *Le Gone du Chaâba* d'Azouz Begag." In *L'Ecriture décentrée: La langue de l'Autre dans le roman contemporain,* ed. Michel Laronde, 109–21. Paris: L'Harmattan, 1996.

Swamy, Vinay. "Should Paradise Be Private? Cultural and Fictive Constructs of National Identity in Two Novels by Azouz Begag." In *Die Kinder der Immigration/Les Enfants de l'immigration,* ed. Ernstpeter Ruhe, 217–31. Würzburg: Königshausen & Neumann, 1999.

Tamba, Said. "Imagination et immigration: A la mémoire de l'ami d'outre-Atlantique." *Information sur les sciences sociales* 31, no. 1 (1992): 153–57.

Tarrow, Susan. "I/ID/Identity: Shuffling the Cards." *French Politics and Society* 9, no. 2 (spring 1991): 53–60.